MYTHIC-SYMBOLIC LANGUAGE
AND PHILOSOPHICAL ANTHROPOLOGY

A Constructive Interpretation of the Thought of Paul Ricœur

MYTHIC-SYMBOLIC LANGUAGE
AND PHILOSOPHICAL ANTHROPOLOGY

A Constructive Interpretation of the Thought of Paul Ricœur

by

DAVID M. RASMUSSEN

MARTINUS NIJHOFF / THE HAGUE / 1971

ISBN 90 247 5087 3

PRINTED IN THE NETHERLANDS

ACKNOWLEDGEMENTS

I am indebeted to Paul Ricoeur for having created the body of thought to which this book is critically and constructively addressed and for choosing to respond to it with an essay. That essay should be read as a further elaboration of hermeneutic phenomenology. I must also thank Mircea Eliade whose insights into myth and symbol initially stimulated this writer's interest. To Sandra and Anne, my gratitude.

DAVID M. RASMUSSEN
Department of Philosophy
February 1, 1971   Boston College

TABLE OF CONTENTS

INTRODUCTION

This book will attempt to achieve a constructive and positive correlation between mythic-symbolic language and philosophical anthropology. It is intended as a reflection on the philosophical accomplishment of Paul Ricoeur. The term mythic-symbolic language in this context means the language of the multivalent symbol given in the myth with its psychological and poetic counterparts. The term symbol is not conceived as an abstract sign as it is used in symbolic logic, but rather as a concrete phenomenon – religious, psychological, and poetic. The task inherent in this correlation is monumental when one considers the dual dilemma of problematic and possibility which is at its heart. The problematic arises out of the apparent difficulty presented by the so-called challenge of modernity which seems to require the elimination of mythic-symbolic language as an intelligible mode of communication. Mythic-symbolic language is sometimes eliminated because in a world molded by abstract conceptualizations of science, such a language is thought to be unintelligible. The claim is that its "primitive" explanations have been transcended by our modernity. Others believe that the problem of mythic-symbolic language is the problem of the myth. If the mythic forms of language could be eliminated, the truth of such language could be preserved through its translation into an intelligible mode of discourse.

The problematic is heightened further by the relation of considerations of language to philosophical anthropology. Any consideration of language involves a related view of the nature of man. It has been suggested that contemporary men are somehow different from their predecessors in the sense that they no longer require a mythic and symbolic mode of discourse. It is claimed that they live in a "scientific age" which can be contrasted with a "mythic age." Therefore, men who are influenced primarily by this contemporary scientific-historical epoch can ascribe no longer to the outmoded language of the symbol.

On the immediate level, this book is simply an argument for the correlation between mythic-symbolic language and the nature of man, predicated on the assumption that any view of language will bear with it a correlative interpretation of the nature of man. For example, to claim that the goal of language is to achieve univocal, transparent concepts, as Wittgenstein does in the *Tractatus*, assumes that language must be formulated in such a way that it expresses the quintessence of human rationality. To claim, like Ernst Cassirer and Susanne Langer, that language, one of a number of symbolic forms, is composed of discursive symbols, has as its basis and consequence, the assumption that man is primarily homo symbolicus, a symbol forming being. In each case a correlation between language and the nature of man is made, and although that correlation may not be stated explicitly, it is assumed implicitly.[1]

But the argument for this correlation cannot be launched on neutral ground, for if anything, this correlation has been stated negatively in modern thought. A positive correlation is possible. This correlation would affirm mythic-symbolic language in its primary form and in its secondary (hermeneutically interpreted) form associated with a philosophical anthropology, an understanding of man which requires such language. In a sense the issue is the necessity of a mythic-symbolic mode of discourse. Does mythic-symbolic language have any specific and necessary role, or is it better rejected in favor of another type of language?

This issue is raised in part as the consequence of a study of the works of Paul Ricoeur, the subject of this book. The question is the working question that has resulted from a study of his works. Why should a philosopher consider mythic-symbolic language at all? This is the challenge of Ricoeur's thought. Why does mythic-symbolic language present something to a philosophic investigation that is thought to be unattainable otherwise? This is the question a study of Ricoeur raises. Here we confront the question of a hermeneutic. The interpretation of an author, a living author, is perhaps the most difficult of tasks. Interpretation really begins when the interpreter opens the first book, as this interpreter did some years ago with *Fallible Man*. At that point

---

[1] Ludwig Wittgenstein, *Tractatus Logico-Philosophicus*, trans. by D. F. Pears and B. F. McGuiness (London: Routledge and Kegan Paul, 1963); Ernst Cassirer, *The Philosophy of Symbolic Forms* (3 vols.; New Haven and London: Yale University Press, 1953–57); Susanne K. Langer, *Philosophy in a New Key* (New York and Toronto: Mentor Book, 1951).

the interpreter begins to formulate his question. Like the symbol, Ricoeur's thought is multivalent. Consequently, this interpretation cannot bring together all the facets, all the meanings, of this prolific writer. In the last analysis, all the interpretations for all of the writings are given through a reading of the basic works. Our hermeneutic of this author is a modest task. However, the problem to which this hermeneutic found solution in Ricoeur's works is not a modest one. Ricoeur's thought raises the question of meaning in a new way. It suggests a new direction for philosophy culminating in a phenomenological hermeneutic.

A positive correlation between mythic-symbolic language and philosophical anthropology is that reflection which is derived as a consequence of reading the works of Paul Ricoeur. If there is a sense of collaboration between author and interpreter it is this problem that the author helped this interpreter to clarify.

There is a central theme in the writings of Paul Ricoeur. Fundamentally his thought emanates from the question "who is man"? Methodologically his works represent a systematic quest for the resources for understanding the nature of man. The problem is massive. It raises the question of the resources for human meaning in our so-called contemporary, modern and often nihilistic society. Are there sources of meaning beyond those which are autonomous and self-created? Are the radical existentialists and the nihilists correct when they suggest that the only sources for human meaning are those which are self-constructed? A reader of Ricoeur's works would suggest that they are not. Herein one finds an argument against that kind of thinking. As Ricoeur has stated so aptly, if the first Copernican revolution in philosophy was the discovery of the self in knowing, the second must be the discovery of that which is given to the self. It is perhaps this generation that will discover the limits of autonomy by moving beyond it. Mythic-symbolic language provides us with a given for this second Copernican revolution.

Such a movement in philosophical reflection is not simply progressive, futuristic, and eschatological; rather, it is something of a process of anamnesis. It is not simply by the creation of meaning, but also by its recovery that we can arrive at a philosophical anthropology. It is this understanding that a prolonged reflection on Ricoeur's thought gives us. It is this understanding that a hermeneutic of the symbol gives us: discursive and non-discursive, latent and meaningful, multivalent and enigmatic. An enquiry into its meaning may tell us something that contemporary societies have forgotten.

This approach to the writings of Paul Ricoeur incorporates a two-fold attempt to understand both its methodological transformations and the manner in which the central problem of the will with its associated problems of freedom and limitation develop. To study Ricoeur's thought is to involve oneself in a kind of methodological dialectic which leads from the threshold of eidetic phenomenology to hermeneutic phenomenology. Ricoeur is a rigorous methodologist. A foremost interpreter of Husserl, he has attempted to move beyond an *eidetic* phenomenology of a Husserlian type (the classical form of phenomenology) to a phenomenology of language incorporating a hermeneutic method. To understand Ricoeur is to understand that methodological transformation. But a method, after all, is that which is designed to meet a set of problems. For Ricoeur the central problem for philosophical anthropology is the will. How does human freedom come to terms with necessity? It is to meet this issue that Ricoeur's methodology first, is established, and second, is transformed. That problem is the central issue of Ricoeur's constructive thought, *Philosophie de la volonté*. In its choice of subject Ricoeur's work becomes something of an exercise in what must be the central issue of post-Kantian continental philosophy. One finds the problem of freedom arising in the Kantian notion of autonomy and the autonomous self creation of value, the necessary free will, coupled with the existential and phenomenological protest against modern forms of determinism in the name of freedom. The problem of limitation is illustrated through the psychological revelation of the unconscious and the modern positivistic interpretations of man. In the last analysis Ricoeur opts for freedom. But it is a realistic view of freedom, a human freedom. It is this attempt to uncover the meaning of freedom, confronted with limitation that drives him beyond the limitations of an eidetic phenomenology (*Le Volontaire et l'involontaire*, translated *Freedom and Nature*) to consideration of the more radical limitation of fallibility (*L'Homme faillible*, translated *Fallible Man*), and finally to the direct human encounter with evil (*La Symbolique du mal*, translated *The Symbolism of Evil*). This problem causes him to turn to a consideration of psychological symbolism (*De l'interprétation: Essai sur Freud*) and finally to the debate with structuralism. It is this problem that causes Ricoeur to move from an eidetic phenomenology to a hermeneutic phenomenlogy which focuses upon language.

Ricoeur's hermeneutic of language complements modern philosophical discussions of language. His formulation, the symbol invites thought, may be welcomed by ordinary language philosophers for it represents not an attempt to reformulate language, but to think from language. Ricoeur adds his own distinctive perspective to that discussion. His contribution (to date) is not to be found in a consideration of language generally, but in the hermeneutic of a special type of language – the language of symbol and myth.

Finally, the structure of this essay is dictated by a notion of a hermeneutic circle. It begins with a problematic, it incorporates an analysis, and finally it returns to that problematic by attempting to construct a solution to it. This discussion begins with a consideration of the correlation of mythic-symbolic language and philosophical anthropology in the works of Rudolf Bultmann. The reasons for that discussion are obvious. Bultmann's thought has dominated the hermeneutic discussion for a generation. His thought, however, leads to a negative correlation of the central problematic of this essay. Second, the examination turns to the methodological side of Ricoeur's thought to develop his major methodological transition from eidetic phenomenology to hermeneutic phenomenology. Third, on the basis of this methodological understanding, the movement is to the central problem of Ricoeur's thought, the attempt to construct a global anthropology through a consideration of the dialectic of human freedom and human limitation, that is, the problem of the will. In these first two discussions of Ricoeur's constructive work the foundation for the constructive correlation we are seeking begins to emerge. Fourth, the discussion turns to the more recent writings of Paul Ricoeur to show how the methodological and constructive foundations of *The Philosophy of the Will* have developed into an entire philosophic program, particularly in relation to his consideration of Freud and the problem of structuralism. Finally the hermeneutic circle is completed by returning to the initial problematic. Having established the problematic, having thought through the writings of Paul Ricoeur, it is incumbent upon the writer to construct a positive solution to that problematic. A positive correlation between mythic-symbolic language and philosophical anthropology is offered. The final discussion is not an attempt to think beyond Ricoeur; rather, it is an attempt to think in response to his thought.

A NEGATIVE CORRELATION BETWEEN
MYTHIC-SYMBOLIC LANGUAGE AND
THE NATURE OF MAN

A. FROM LANGUAGE TO SPECIAL LANGUAGE

A paradigm of the study of myth, namely the work of Rudolf Bultmann, has been chosen to begin this reflection. The discussion of his
work is necessary and important because it presents a primary example
of recent treatments of that subject. Further, Bultmann's hermeneutic
has been the predominant example of contemporary treatments of
myth. In fact, Bultmann's hermeneutic has been the central one for
philosophical thinking about myth. If, therefore, the ultimate claim
shall be that myth and symbol may be a resource for philosophical
thinking, the discussion must begin here. Such a hermeneutic is problematic. It is also possible that it is symptomatic of the way language
has been treated generally in contemporary discussions.

The problem represented by inquiry into the exigencies of myth and
symbol is initially a linguistic one for, although it has often been fashionable to disassociate myth from language, myths are embedded in
words and symbols and are expressed as well as seen. In a sense there
is no experiencing, at least of the kind that can be remembered, that
is non-linguistic. I have no experience of myself, no experience of the
"I" that I am apart from the linguist tools which allow me to convey
that experience to myself. Equally, I have no experience of another
apart from the givenness of the language which allows me to convey that
other to myself as person or thing. Even my ability to think, to reflect,
would be totally lost if it were not for the medium of language, that
vessel which contains my thoughts. Indeed, language is like one's
body: poor, inadequate, unable always to do what one wants it to do,
and yet it is the very possibility for the expression both of the fulness
of one's being and whatever reality one chooses to describe. Even when
I reflect about my visual encounter with a painting I must resort to

language to convey the meaning of that encounter. In phenomenological terms the *Cogito* is embedded within language in the same sense that thought is impossible without language.

There are different ways of approaching language inclusive of different heuristic devices employed to understand it. Language, whether mythic and metaphorical, logical and rigorous, transparent and conceptually clear, is generally defined as having a common set of properties which both limit and provide the possibility for its various usages. Epistemologically conceived, this abstract realm in which one conceives the term language is a realm of potentiality, for each actual usage given in language conceived as a whole. In order to use language it is necessary that this body of givenness is potentially present in order to be actualized. It is this givenness which conditions my speaking as well as my understanding and in general my thinking. Simply, in order for any kind of communication to be possible it is necessary for there to be this realm of potential usage and meaning. But in order for language to be used it is necessary that it be more than an abstract body of potentiality.

Language is more than a system of signs with a certain grammatical structure because the use of language implies a user of language. Language never becomes actual apart from the speaker who makes this body of potentiality actual through the act of communicating, or the writer who uses language to create new modes of meaning through the reconstitution of the potentiality of language in the concrete creation of a novel, a script, or a poem. For each, language is something given as the fundamental modality through which the creative act takes place, but in each case the actualization of language is the accomplishment of the one who reconstitutes language by bringing it into the focus of a creative subject. Therefore, the *meaning* of language is to be understood through the subject who correlates the potential givenness of language with the actual use of language. It can be said that a philosophy which centers itself in language must deal with its constitution through a human subject.

Two propositions may be suggested, the first negative, the second positive. First, a philosophy of language ought not consider language in itself if it is to truly deal with the interpretation of language. Second, a philosophy of language correlates the potentiality of language with its concrete usage by a human subject.

This approach to language is phenomenological in the sense that it is concerned primarily with the *interpretation* of language as it is consti-

tuted by man. This implies that an investigation into the total body
of language is at least at this point not possible because such an investigation would only conceive language as potential. When language
becomes actual it becomes a special mode of discourse appropriate to a
particular realm of human experience. Language as such is constituted by taking on special characteristics. The point here is that when I
enter a physicist's laboratory I am not simply expected to play a game,
but instead I am expected to speak about a particular kind of experience.
The language I use will be correlated with that particular kind of
experience and I will know how to use the language if I have had some
experience of the problems and solutions germane to that discipline.
Equally, if I read a poem I am invited to experience through the language of the poem the poetic vision. It is true that both the poet and
the physicist are drawing from a common potentiality of language
with certain grammatical rules etc., but it is also true that as language
is constituted by a human subject it distinguishes itself and hence it is
possible to speak of linguistic variations, that is, a scientific language, a
poetic language.

In the following discussion reference will be made to only one dimension of language, a "special language" namely, mythic-symbolic
language. In the context of the discussion of the philosophy of language in general, mythic-symbolic language is uniquely the creation of
the poetic, religious, and on occasion the psychological mind. In a
sense, it is the kind of language that has to be believed to be understood because if one fails to enter into the poetic or religious vision, one
fails to grasp the meaning of the poem or myth. But it is precisely
this kind of language that has not been believed and therefore it is
classified with the unreal, meaningless and inadequate expressions of
contemporary men. It is, of course, a truism that reductionist systems
devised from theoretical discoveries in other areas have been applied to
mythic-symbolic language as the conceptual framework appropriate to
understanding. The result has been disastrous for it has meant that the
kind of language that relies on metaphor, the image, the story, etc.
is logically inferior to modes of discourse which are products of re-
fined abstract theoretical frameworks. The reversal of this tendency of
western thinking is just beginning, however, and it is perhaps possible
now to inquire into the particular properties of this special language
as it applies to religion, literature, etc. The technical problem is whether
or not it is possible to create the kind of heuristic structure to interpret
this distinctive kind of language without destroying it.

By considering a representative theorist whose works on myth are understood as paradigmatic of the central problem which modern western thinkers have had with myth, it will be possible to see negatively the hurdles to be jumped if myth is to be established with some integrity as a special language.

B. BULTMANN: HERMENEUTICS AND THE NATURE OF MAN

This discussion deals with only a segment of the entire range of Bultmann's thought. The initial discussion is preoccupied with two aspects of his thought: (1) his definition of myth associated with the problem of hermeneutics as it pertains to the definition of myth, and (2) the correlate understanding of man related to the definition of myth. Although these two problems are central to his thought, they are not the whole of his thought.

If the position taken with regard to these two issues in Bultmann's thought is critical, it is not without appreciation. He has focused upon a crucial issue for the philosophy of language, that is, the interpretation of primary mythic-symbolic language. Bultmann has shown that whatever one makes of myth is dependent upon an associated understanding of man. Inasmuch as myth is a mode of discourse, he has made the problem of mythic-symbolic language central. Whatever the critical analysis of Bultmann may be, it is made with a sense of indebtedness to him for having raised the problems that are at issue in this discussion.

But the critical problems must be raised. It is our task to point out the limitations of the definition of primary mythic-symbolic language that Bultmann has chosen and to show how these limitations are supported by a correlative understanding of man. At the point of these limitations, Bultmann is a representative figure, for he sustains a type of thinking about myth and modernity that extends beyond him to more recent exponents. In this sense, the critical focus is on Bultmann.

Finally, criticism is offered for the purpose of construction. The critique allows for the statement of the problem of the essay in a concrete context. It sets the stage for a more adequate view of primary mythic-symbolic discourse associated with a different understanding of man.

I. *The Definition of Myth*

For Bultmann, religious phenomena occur most simply in the form of myth, or as the mythology present in the New Testament. "The cosmology of the New Testament is essentially mythical in character."[1] In the Bultmannian context, myth constitutes the "given" for the study of religion with the consequence that it is from this point that the hermeneutical task begins. It is about the phenomenon of myth that Bultmann goes on to make his most important axiological judgment. For Bultmann, myth is an invalid form. Myth is invalid because it simply represents the cosmology of a pre-scientific age. This being the case, it is already pre-determined that modern man is incapable of understanding it. As Bultmann says:

No man can accept a view of the world by his own volition – it is already determined for him by his place in history.[2]
...Man's knowledge and mastery of the world have advanced to such an extent through science and technology that it is no longer possible for anyone seriously to hold the New Testament view of the world – in fact, there is no one who does.[3]

Bultmann claims that history has proved mythology to be untrue. "The mythical eschatology is untenable for the simple reason that the parousia of Christ never took place as the New Testament expected."[4]

Must one, as a consequence of this understanding of myth, dismiss mythic-symbolic phenomena in their totality and opt for a self-understanding presented solely dependent on the zeitgeist of the contemporary world? Or does myth contain within its obscure expressions an undismissable truth? To answer these questions, we become involved in a second set of assumptions regarding mythic-symbolic phenomena. These assumptions conclude that, although the form of the structure which embodies mythic symbolic phenomena is invalid, the content is valid. The first assumption is that the intentionality of myth, or its purpose, is not to present an objective vision of the world, but to present man's true understanding of himself in the world in which he lives. Secondly:

Myth is an expression of man's conviction that the origin and purpose of the world in which he lives are to be sought not within it but beyond it – that is beyond the realm of the known and tangible reality – and that this realm is per-

---

[1] Rudolf Bultmann, *Kerygma and Myth* (1st Harper Torchbook ed.; New York: Harper and Brothers, 1961), p. 1.
[2] *Ibid.*, p. 3.
[3] *Ibid.*, p. 4.
[4] *Ibid.*, p. 5.

petually dominated and menaced by those mysterious powers which are at its source and limit.[5]

The following conclusions can be drawn from these two assumptions:

The real purpose of myth is to speak of a transcendent power which controls the world and man, but that purpose is obscured by the terms in which it is expressed.

The basis of the Bultmannian enterprise of demythologization is constituted by the assumptions that religious phenomena are primarily myth: that the form in which such language manifests itself obscures the reality that it attempts to present. If it is possible to find a way to free the intention of myth from the rigidity of its expression, one may discover the true and real message contained in mythic-symbolic phenomena. Myth then presents a fundamental problem, a hermeneutical problem. Myth raises the question of understanding.

Over the years of his productive life Bultmann has held to this definition fairly consistently. As late as 1958, in the book *Jesus Christ and Mythology*, he states:

It is often said that mythology is a primitive science, the intention of which is to explain phenomena and incidents which are strange, curious, surprising, or frightening, by attributing them to supernatural causes, to gods or to demons.[6]

By form, he means the part of myth that is primitive science, to be distinguished from the intention which is existential. When demythologized, the form is not myth but kerygma. The question of how one understands myth becomes central. This leads to a discussion of the problem of hemeneutics.

2. *The Problem of Hermeneutics*

For Bultmann, the breakthrough in the history of the problem of hermeneutics occurs with Romanticism and its exponent, Friedrich Schleiermacher. Schleiermacher accepted as valid the equation of hermeneutics with rules, but he was critical of that position because it was not adequate to the full understanding of literary texts. It was Schleiermacher who added to the already established tradition of hermeneutics the application of the Romantic imagination to the problem of interpretation, a point from which Dilthey drew some of his significant implications later. Bultmann places himself firmly within this tradition of Romantic interpretation. The Romantic criticism of

---

[5] Bultmann, *Kerygma and Myth*, pp. 10–11.

[6] Rudolf Bultmann, *Jesus Christ and Mythology* (New York: Charles Scribner's Sons, 1958), pp. 18–19.

the hermeneutic tradition was simply that hermeneutical rules are not adequate because they fail to capture the living character of the phenomena they are attempting to interpret. Hermeneutics becomes the attempt to understand in this sense; neither formalistic logic nor stylistic interpretation is adequate to grasp fully the meaning of a phenomenon. The addition of the Romantic imagination is this: *the criterion of participation or subjectivity*. As Bultmann states:

To the comprehension of the "external form" must be joined that of the "internal form.". . . Hence interpreting is a "copying," a "modelling" in its live relationship to the process of literary production itself. Comprehension becomes its "own reproduction of the live nexus of thoughts." But such "reproduction" is possible because the "individuality of the exegete and that of the author do not stand opposed to each other as two facts which cannot be compared." Rather it is that both have been formed on the basis of human nature in general and by this the social life of men is made possible for purposes of speech and understanding.[7]

To put it succinctly, as Dilthey did:

The conditioning of understanding "lies in the fact that nothing can appear in an unfamiliar, individual form of expression which was not also contained in the quality of living that comprehends it."[8]

The reason for the possibility of understanding is contained in the fact that texts are written by men, and man as such is capable of communication. Generally, what Bultmann discovers in the contribution of Dilthey and Schleiermacher he recapitulates as his own. To the conception of hermeneutics as rules of interpretation must be added the conception of hermeneutics as participation. This conception is launched on the assumption that both the text interpreted, and the interpreter, participate in the common historical consciousness of the human.

The hermeneutical position of Bultmann is to be seen in direct continuity with that of the Romantic school of Schleiermacher and Dilthey. Bultmann goes beyond them, not by departing from them, but by extending their own thought. Hermeneutics gains specificity in the Bultmannian context by what he calls the "putting of the question." He states:

So far as Dilthey *characterizes the relationship between author and expositor* as the conditioning factor for the possibility of comprehension of the text he has in fact laid bare the presupposition of all interpretation which has comprehension as its basis.[9]

---

[7] Rudolf Bultmann, *Essays, Philosophical and Theological* (London: SCM Press Ltd., 1955), pp. 237-38.
[8] *Ibid.*, p. 238.
[9] *Ibid.*, p. 240.

For Bultmann then, the problem of hermeneutics is "simply a question of determining this presupposition more accurately."[10] The problem of hermeneutics may be specified by inquiry into the question of the investigating subject with the consequence that the way one asks the question of the text is conditioned by some prior understanding of the subject. The basic presupposition of the subject is the pre-understanding implicit in the question being asked. The way a text is interpreted will be determined to a large degree by the question that the inquirer brings to the text.

Certainly, Bultmann must be credited for this extension of the process of interaction between subject and object begun through the distinctive work of Dilthey and Schleiermacher. It seems apparent that one's understanding and experience of music would color the interpretation of a musical text; one's prior understanding of art would condition the understanding of a particular painting. It follows that texts would be interpreted in various ways in accord with the particular questions put to them. In Bultmann's interpretive scheme there are four such possibilities. Texts are interpreted in order to reconstruct past history and this interpretation will always be determined by the view the interpreter has of past history. Second, the object of interpretation may be established by psychological interest, thirdly, by aesthetic interest, and finally, and most important, by an existential interest, in which case the inquiry is governed by the possibilities offered for man's existence.

The Bultmannian hermeneutical position consists of a concern to go beyond pure rules of grammatical interpretation to the Romantic position. The Romantic position construed the process of hermeneutics as an interrelation of subject and object, which adds specificity by examining the nature of the question put to the text. Through this putting of the question, Bultmann presents the key to his hermeneutic position. The concern for historical understanding in the context of historical relativism is the problem of the welfare of one's own existence. The question of the salvatory possibilities for man in the comtemporary scientific world is the hermeneutical question which brings us right back to the mythic-symbolic phenomenon itself. The burden that mythic-symbolic phenomena must bear is that of answering the question of man's existence. By returning to mythic-symbolic phenomena, having clarified the hermeneutic, we will be able to watch its operation.

When we left the earlier discussion of myth, the problem was how to

[10] Bultmann, *Essays*, p. 241.

free the content of myth from the form of myth. The proper test of the
hermeneutics is an examination of whether or not it is capable of fulfilling the prescribed task to be accomplished by the proper establishment of the question, specifically, asking the soteriological question
about one's own existence. It is possible to speak of two languages, one
primary language of myth which remains unintelligible, and a secondary language of interpretation which is construed in primarily existential categories. The bridge between the two languages is the hermeneutical question with the consequence that a demythologized form of
interpretation replaces the primary language of myth.

The hermeneutical question is applied to religious phenomena. In
other words, the application of the method of demythologization to
Christian and Jewish apocalyptic myths provides the interpreter with
these results: (1) a description of the life of faith, or in its demythologized existential form, a description of eschatological and authentic
existence. Predominant in this scheme are the demythologized equi-
valents of the mythological terms "grace of God" and "forgiveness of
sins." Properly interpreted, and therefore, demythologized, the former –
grace of God – means love opening up the future under the rubric life
rather than death. The latter – forgiveness of sins – means deliverance
from the bondage of the past. Further investigation reveals that the
life of faith is understood as life under the eschatological form of the
myth or eschatological existence, which, in its demythologized form,
means life as a new creature. Again, a significant probing of the various
stages of the New Testament illustrates variations on the extent to
which eschatological forms are internalized inasmuch as they are ap-
propriated for particular themes of personal existence. The method of
demythologization is an implicit form within the New Testament itself.
One finds a relative demythologization with the consequence that the
hermeneutical method is grounded in the material itself and finds its
best exemplification in the Fourth Gospel. (2) The second factor implicit in the mythological phenomena which the hermeneutical question will reveal is the demythologization of the event of Jesus Christ
examined particularly in relation to the cross and the resurrection. If
one accepts with Bultmann the assumption that the cross and the resurrection are the representative symbols of the event of Jesus Christ,
we must assume that the cross is a mythical phenomenon which, when
demythologized, means a release from the powers that control his own
being.

In its redemptive aspect the cross of Christ is no mere mythical event, but a historical (*geschichtlich*) fact originating in the historical (*historisch*) event which is the crucifixion of Jesus.[11]

The cross is the judgment and deliverance of man. As judgment and deliverance are inseparable, so the cross cannot be separated from the resurrection.

Cross and resurrection form a single, indivisible cosmic event which brings judgment to the world and opens up for men the possibility of authentic life.[12]

This is nothing other than an opportunity for self-understanding in the context of the sole reality of authentic existence.

In summary: the mythic-symbolic phenomenon is judged a priori as invalid because it fails to participate in the contemporary world, thus the form of the myth obscures the possible truth embodied within it. The myth requires the necessary development of a hermeneutic which will release the authentic content of the myth from the inauthentic form of the myth. An investigation into the history of the problem of hermeneutics reveals the necessary criticism of hermeneutics interpreted as rules and an acceptance and agreement with the Romantic assumption that the object interpreted and the subject interpreting participate in a mutual historical consciousness which is the precondition of the hermeneutic task. This task is defined further in terms of the pre-understanding which determines the "putting of the question." The hermeneutic, now fully developed and returned to the subject matter, reveals a life of faith, which, when re-interpreted, means authentic existence articulated through a demythologized understanding of the cross and resurrection. This is Bultmann's hermeneutic brought full circle from uninterpreted mythic-symbolic phenomenon to interpreted mythic-symbolic phenomenon.

C. THE PROBLEM OF A NEGATIVE DEFINITION OF MYTHIC-SYMBOLIC LANGUAGE

The aim of demythologizing is "not to eliminate mythological statements but to interpret them."[13] However, any interpretation of myth depends upon a prior definition of myth. Our critique shall be directed at Bultmann's etiological definition of the primary mythic-symbolic

---

[11] Bultmann, *Kerygma and Myth*, p. 37.
[12] *Ibid.*, p. 39.
[13] Bultmann, *Jesus Christ and Mythology*, p. 18.

form. For Bultmann, the form (language) of myth is etiological while the intention of myth is existential. Two problems arise from this definition. First, the etiological definition of myth is fundamentally negative. Second, myth so defined is juxtaposed to contemporary science.

The problem arising from an etiological definition of myth is one of verification because the initial juxtaposition is between myth as primitive science and modern science. If modern science offers a better explanation for natural events, myth etiologically defined must be rejected in the name of "modern man" who cannot accept these primitive explanations. So defined, myth cannot be verified, for its truth value cannot be retained as myth.

This etiological definition creates a hermeneutical dilemma. As interpreter of myth, Bultmann's solution is to separate the etiological form from the existential intention of this primary mythic-symbolic form. The language of myth must be translated into existential language to be sustained as meaningful. By so doing, he claims to have freed myth from the pseudo-offense that myth as an etiological form might present. The hermeneutic solution is to translate myth into statements that can be affirmed. It is assumed that contemporary existential language is verifiable and can function as a proper replacement for mythic language. But the important consequence of the Bultmannian definition is that myth can be affirmed in intention only. Verification occurs only on the basis of a fairly complete translation into existential language.

This position on the verification of mythic language, a fundamental one, has within it the peculiar contradiction that the validity of mythic discourse occurs only through the rejection of mythic language in its primary form. That is perhaps the price of an etiological definition of myth. For mythic language is not a valid language but a language which obscures. "Myths give wordly objectivity to that which is unworldy."[14] Hence the only solution to this problem, if one wishes to follow the Bultmannian proposal, is the translation of mythical discourse into another form. If the Gospel is to be made relevant for Bultmann, it is necessary that the interpreter "undertake the task of stripping that Kerygma from its mythological framework."[15] The Kerygma is valid language; myth is not.

The consequence of an etiological definition of myth and its associated hermeneutic is reductionism. Mythic language is judged invalid.

[14] Bultmann, *Jesus Christ and Mythology*, p. 19.
[15] Bultmann, *Kerygma and Myth*, p. 3.

The only way to establish the validity of such language is through translation. Reduction from one language to another becomes the mode and style of the hermeneutic. Reductionism has as its associated principle the elimination of mythic discourse.

From this perspective it seems difficult to find a means of verifying mythic discourse because the etiological definition makes of myth an a priori invalid form. The question becomes one of verifying mythic discourse as a primary form. But, if myth is etiologically defined, this is impossible. This is the first hermeneutic problem presented by the etiological definition. Even more difficult, is the fact that this definition places the would-be defender of mythic language in the precarious position of arguing for the elimination of his own primary discourse. It is necessary to state, in justice to Bultmann, that his argument is constructed for hermeneutic and theological reasons. The price of the argument is the elimination of myth as a primary mode of discourse.

This analysis and critique allows the following conclusions: (1) Etiologically defined myth cannot be verified for two reasons. First, because it conflicts with modern scientific causal explanations, and second, because it objectifies and makes immanent that which is by nature transcendent. (2) This position leads necessarily and inevitably to the development of a hermeneutic which requires the negation of mythic-symbolic discourse in its primary form.

One question remains. Can one transcend the etiological definition of myth? We assume that this is necessary if one is to sustain the validity of mythic-symbolic discourse in any form.[16]

A doctrine of man can influence a definition of primary mythic-symbolic discourse in two ways. First, the acceptance or rejection of mythic discourse will depend upon whether or not one assumes that a mythic mentality is a product of a particular historical period with the associated assumption that contemporary man has "come of age" and is, therefore, beyond that historical period. The alternative assumption is that myth is a constitutive expression of human consciousness regardless of the particular period in which it was produced. Second, anyone who has any investment in mythic discourse will want to show either the significance of myth for an understanding of man or how one may

---

[16] In an excellent summary of the scope and direction of the so-called "New Hermeneutics." James M. Robinson states: "Bultmann's program of demythologizing is embedded in a specific view of language as the objectification of understanding, an objectification that is itself contrary to the understanding seeking expression in it." *The New Hermeneutic*, ed. by James M. Robinson and John B. Cobb, Jr. (2 vols.; New York: Harper and Row, Publishers, 1964), II, p. 37.

transcend the limitations of this form. As one who has seen that the liberal attempt to separate the non-mythological kernel from the mythological husk is simply impossible, Bultmann has recognized that as given the language of the New Testament is mythological. He has a basic position on both of these issues.

A distinction can be made between an historical-evolutionary view of mythic forms and a fully phenomenological view of the functions and role of myth. In the conclusion of the book, *Primitive Mentality*, Levy-Bruhl attempts to draw a basic distinction between the so-called primitive mind and the contemporary European mind. He states:

> In short, our (the modern European) mentality is above all "conceptual," and theirs (the primitive mind) hardly at all so. It is, therefore, extremely difficult, if not impossible, for a European, even if he tries, and even if he knows the natives' language to *think* as they do, although he may *speak* as they do.[17]

His point was:

> Almost unconsciously, the European makes use of abstract thought, and his language has made simple logical processes so easy to him that they entail no effort. With primitives both thought and language are almost exclusively concrete by nature.[18]

The primitive with his mythical mentality could be contrasted with modern man and his logical scientific mentality. Levy-Bruhl was expressing a point of view that had been fashionable among some anthropologists, historians of religion, and, one might add, theologians for more than a generation.

No more dramatic reversal of this view can be expressed than in Levi-Strauss' essay on the structural study of myth:

> Prevalent attempts to explain alleged differences between the so-called primitive mind and scientific thought have resorted to qualitative differences between the working processes of the mind in both cases, while assuming that the entities which they were studying remained very much the same. If our interpretation is correct, we are led toward a completely different view – namely, that the kind of logic in mythical thought is as rigorous as that of modern science, and that the difference lies, not in the quality of the intellectual process, but in the nature of the things to which it is applied.[19]

The former view juxtaposes the primitive and the modern on the basis of an historical-evolutionary model for understanding man. The latter view finds such a juxtaposition unnecessary on the basis of a structural

---

[17] Lucien Levy-Bruhl, *Primitive Mentality*, trans. by Lilian A. Clare (Boston: Beacon Press, 1966), pp. 433–34.

[18] *Ibid.*, p. 433.

[19] Claude Levi-Strauss, *Structural Anthropology* (New York and London: Basic Books, Inc., 1963), pp. 229–30.

model. Myth in the first view is understood as the product of a particular pre-scientific age. Myth in the second view is seen as a constitutive
product of human consciousness characteristic of any age.

Bultmann employs a distinction between the modern and the pre-
modern, but the manner in which he does so requires clarification.
First, the distinction between modern and pre-modern is used to illustrate the dilemma that mythical material presents to modern man.
Second, Bultmann has to reject the distinction in part because the radical contrast between myth and modernity, so defined, will result in a
complete rejection, not only of the form of myth, but also its intention.
Hence, the former view is modified.

The initial definition of myth and the problematic it presents, is one
which accepts a fairly complete distinction between a modern and pre-
modern mentality. This is presented in Bultmann's work by the juxtaposition of contrasting *Weltanschauungen*. A pre-modern world view,
to be contrasted with a modern one, sets forth a cosmology which is
essentially mythological in character.

The whole conception of the world which is presupposed in the preaching of
Jesus, as in the New Testament generally is mythological; i.e., the conception of
the world as being structured in three stories, heaven, earth, and hell; the conception of the intervention of supernatural powers in the course of events; the
conception of miracles, especially the conception of supernatural power in the
inner life of the soul; the conception that man can be tempted and corrupted by
the devil and possessed by evil spirits.[20]

In contrast to this view, Bultmann claims "modern science does not
believe that the course of nature can be interrupted, or, so to speak, per-
forated, by supernatural powers."[21]

Now this understanding of man is certainly credible, for it is true
that contemporary man has difficulty with concepts of heaven, hell,
demons, etc. He is capable of making a distinction between myth and
history for he no longer views the culmination of history as a cataclys-
mic end. Bultmann is correct to the extent that contemporary men
cannot accept the Christian myth literally. My problem with this interpretation comes at the point of the distinction between a mythological
Weltanschauung and a modern scientific one. Bultmann has claimed
that human understanding is determined by a particular world view,
either pre-scientific or scientific. This determination is said to be inevitable. "No man can adopt a view of the world by his own volition –
it is already determined for him by his place in history."[22] We wish to

[20] Bultmann, *Jesus Christ and Mythology*, p. 15
[21] *Ibid.*
[22] Bultmann, *Kerygma and Myth*, p. 3.

question both the logical consistency and the adequacy of this position.

If we are to assume that man can be described adequately by distinguishing two epochs, the first being mythological, while the second is logical, scientific and modern, then, as a consequence, anyone who wishes to defend myth finds it already ruled out as a mode of thought because it cannot be sustained in a modern scientific age. If the argument is pressed for consistency, it would suggest that man, under the modern scientific *Weltanschauung*, has no need to retreat to myth since the explanations provided by myth have been surpassed by the explanations of science. The distinction between logical and pre-logical modes of thought may work very well for one whose presuppositions are positivistic because the relevance of myth to modern man is unimportant from that perspective. Myth is a datum in the history of human consciousness, the relevance of which is ruled out by modern scientific consciousness. Myth is significant for historical interest alone. But if the student of myth is a philosopher of religion, the case is the opposite. If he chooses to press this distinction and force the argument with rigor, the result will be that there is no necessity for defending religious man, the man of mythic age, because he has been surpassed. It is the virtue of Bultmann that he does not follow the argument consistently. At the conclusion of the programmatic essay, Bultmann argues for the retention of the basic terminology of the Christian proclamation; but he argues that this terminology is no longer mythological. Yet, paradoxically, he still wishes to retain terminology like: "The word became flesh," and "the word of God," which he claims as data proclaimed for faith, and therefore, not mythological. [23] That kind of language, ordinarily associated with mythological concepts, is not rejected. Secondly, the modern world-view, which was itself an original criterion for the criticism of myth, is also rejected because modern man, under this world-view, regards himself as a "self-subsistent unity immune from the interference of supernatural powers."[24]

Faith is the abandonment of man's own security and the readiness to find security only in the unseen beyond, in God.[25]

The credibility of this approach to myth, based as it is upon a distinction between the modern and the pre-modern man, is questionable. The consequence of this view is the rejection of mythic language in the name of a presupposed understanding of modern man. This under-

[23] Bultmann, *Kerygma and Myth*, p. 44.
[24] *Ibid.*, p. 7.
[25] Bultmann, *Jesus Christ and Mythology*, p. 40.

standing assumes that modern man is immune to myth. If myth is so conceived, I believe that philosophical reflection on myth is rendered difficult, if not impossible. If mythic language is the product of pre-scientific age, how can reflection on mythic language survive as a legitimate enterprise in a scientific age? If one maintains that contemporary man, under the dominance of a modern world view, is one to whom the pre-modern varieties of myth are no longer relevant, then it does not follow that these concepts are relevant.

Not only is this position inconsistent, but I believe it is inadequate. This position is inadequate because it rests upon an initial definition of man that assumes that at one period in man's history he was dominated by a mythological type of thinking while at another his thought may be dominated by non-mythological concepts. But this theory simply does not account for the variety of expressions of human consciousness that is present in any age. Karl Jasper's criticism of Bultmann is relevant. He states:

"The myth" says Bultmann, "is to be interpreted, divested of its mythological garb, and transposed into a truth valid for today..." I deny this. Mythological thinking is not a thing of the past, but characterizes man in any epoch.[26]

In our terms, Bultmann has taken an etiological view of myth which juxtaposes myth and science and undergirded that view by the concept of two world-views. It seems that a better anthropological model for understanding myth would be one that understands it as a dimension of consciousness which is a permanently valid form of thought. At this juncture we find support among figures such as Claude Levi-Strauss, Mircea Eliade, and Paul Ricoeur who have found it necessary to go beyond the limitations of the distinction between the logical and the pre-logical to affirm myth as a distinctive dimension of human thought.

The aspect or segment of Bultmann's thought analyzed here is predicated upon a series of inter-related judgments which can be submitted to critical evaluation. The problem arises at the point of Bultmann's use of two hypotheses; the first assuming that primary mythic-symbolic language can survive an etiological definition; and the second contending that it is necessary to juxtapose primitive and modern experience. What makes the Bultmannian program for demythologizing confusing is his inability to hold his position consistently. If he held it consistently, there would be no reason to carry on the philosophical task.

[26] Karl Jaspers and Rudolf Bultmann, *Myth and Christianity* (New York: The Noonday Press, 1958), p. 15.

For by definition, contemporary man must find myth irrelevant to his self-understanding. Bultmann finds it necessary to retain the symbols God, Jesus Christ, Church, Grace, word of God, faith, etc., as mythological residue, which, although he claims they are not myth, cannot be correlated exactly with contemporary scientific experience. If the position is inconsistent, it must be held as such. It is possible to suggest that the virtue of Bultmann is his inconsistency.

The illogicality of an argument is not Bultmann's responsibility alone. He is simply a representative figure par excellence. One finds the argument expressed in many ways. If the chief motif of contemporary experience is secularity, meaning the tendency of contemporary man to drift away from religious belief, it is difficult to see how myth and symbolism can be sustained in the context of secularism. If contemporary experience is characterized by the loss or the death of God and the lack of religious experience, it does not make much sense to argue for the retention of that experience.

Bultmann, as a representative figure, places us on the horns of a basic dilemma which may be stated in two propositions: (1) *The etiological definition of primary mythic-symbolic language requires the negation of primary mythic-symbolic language.* The hermeneutic method of demythologization is designated to meet this problem but it cannot be pressed to its most radical limit, that is, total demythologization. To do so would result in total elimination of all primary mythic-symbolic forms with the consequence that if such forms can be eliminated so easily, the primary mythic-symbolic form has little validity in the first place. (2) *The distinction between the pre-modern and the modern results in the negation of the pre-modern in the name of the modern.* If the correlate of primary mythic-symbolic language is pre-modern experience, the case for the validity of primary mythic-symbolic discourse, or its contribution to contemporary experience, is difficult to make. We find that this position is held inconsistently by Bultmann. Ultimately the claim is made that factors important to pre-modern mythic experience are also important to modern experience. Bultmann finally contends that the problem with modern man is that he closes himself off from these pre-modern possibilities.

Factors of consistency or inconsistency may or may not be judged important. Certainly, consistency is not solely the ultimate purpose of every philosophical position; but the kinds of problems toward which lack of consistency points are important and cannot be overlooked. If one takes the position that myth is an invalid form and has to be eliminated because of its invalidity, the value of the study of that kind of language for any purpose may be questioned. If it is maintained that modern experience is qualitatively different from pre-modern experience, then the study of pre-modern experience has only cursory and historical significance.

We have not intended to criticize Bultmann unjustly. But Bultmann's centrality in this discussion cannot be overlooked. However, we do wish to make a very direct and simple point. The reductionism that is implicit in that point of view results, almost inevitably, in the elimination of mythic-symbolic discourse. It does so for very specific anthropological reasons. The problem is this: is there a way in which mythic-symbolic language can be retained as a significant dimension of human meaning? It is with that foundational question that one is able to turn to the thought of Paul Ricoeur.

The argument that we have made with regard to a hermeneutic of myth could be generalized to include other types of thinking about language. Presently there is a rebellion against reductionistic systems among various schools of linguistic analysis. Post-Wittgensteinian thought about language does not attempt to think from a preconceived system of language. Rather, it attempts to think from language without attempting to reform it. In literary theory there is a protest against any theoretical system which would abort the integrity of a literary phenomenon. Among the structural studies of language there are attempts to analyze the structure of a linguistic system as it is. The older attempts to make qualitative distinctions between various linguistic systems have been given up. In other words, support could be marshalled for the first critical thesis of this essay from other studies of language. However, at this point our problem is not the problem of language in general. Our concern is with the specific nature of mythic-symbolic language. The reader is free to make his own parallels and analogies.

II

METHODOLOGICAL PERSPECTIVES: FROM PHENOMENOLOGY TO HERMENEUTIC PHENOMENOLOGY

Freedom, the subject of the final discussion of the first volume of Paul Ricoeur's *Philosophy of the Will*, is defined as solely human, the telos of his philosophical anthropology. Under the methodological rubric of the qualified phenomenological reduction which characterized this work, freedom is presented as a "radical paradox" which balances uneasily in deciding, moving, and consenting . . . the three distinct movements of the will as "incarnate," "contingent," and "motivated," emerging "ceaselessly out of indecision," a "kind of process" arising as a "risk and not from a decree," "gracious" and "spontaneous." Although the thematic properties of Ricoeur's thought are not confined to considerations of freedom alone, this subject presents the reader with the first clue to the emerging combination of issues which coalesce to illustrate the direction and scope of his work.

The struggle to transcend the modern existential vision of man as condemned to finitude provides a second predominant theme. *Fallible Man* opts neither for finitude nor infinitude as the predominant anthropological norm selectively illustrated in a Cartesian paradox, the Platonic myth of the melange, and Pascal's description of man situated between two infinites. Epistemologically, immediate perception is always transcended by language about the thing perceived. The argument concludes with the contention that understanding man as limited to finitude is narrow because language functions in such a way that the finitude of perception is always transcended.

In the concluding essay of *History and Truth*, Ricoeur employs a dialectical method to circumvent the French philosophers who make negativity the primary "ontological" characteristic of man. As with finitude, so with negation, Ricoeur furthers the drive toward fundamental affirmation by locating in the original act of negation, a negation of a negation, and therefore a movement toward primary affirmation. He states:

> ...negativity is the privileged road of the climb back to foundation; ...to dis-
> cover human transcendence in the transgression of point of view, and negativity
> in transcendence; then to discover in this negation a double negation, the se-
> cond negation of point of view as primary negation, and then to discover this
> primary affirmation within negation.[1]

In the original act of consciousness one may discover negation, but negativity can be overcome through a transgression of the finitude of point of view, the primary fact of experience. Negation thus leads to affirmation through the quasi-Hegelian process of a double negation culminating in affirmation. Herbert Spiegelberg has called Ricoeur's phenomenology essentially a philosophy of "affirmation" wherein "the central motif is that of a reconciliation, a reconciliation of man with himself, his body and the world." According to Spiegelberg, Ricoeur's philosophy represents a movement beyond Sartre's philosophy of freedom which is "essentially negation." Ricoeur shares with Gabriel Marcel the desire to affirm man's being-in-the-world as well as his idealistic tendency to emphasize affirmation and transcendence.

Ricoeur's thought may be characterized by a drive toward the *concrete* involving the methodological shift from the techniques of eidetic phenomenology, eidetic reduction, to a concrete hermeneutic program. Abstract considerations of will are replaced by concrete confessions of evil in symbol and myth. The abstract mode of conscious reflection is replaced by concrete considerations of language involving a choice of symbol and myth as the subject matter for philosophic investigation. In symbol and myth the human experience of rupture is presented, while the hermeneutic method explicates that experience. In this sense, the investigation of language represents the final aim of Ricoeur's philosophical anthropology. In his programmatic article, "The Hermeneutics of Symbols and Philosophical Reflection," Ricoeur illustrates the possibilities illuminated through this orientation.

> In the very age in which our language is becoming more precise, more univocal,
> more technical, better suited to those integral formalizations that are called
> precisely "symbolic" logic... it is in this age of discourse that we wish to re-
> charge language, start again from the fullness of language.[2]

Ricoeur's contention is that man's most significant confrontation with

---

[1] Paul Ricoeur, *History and Truth*, trans. by Charles A. Kelbley (Evanston: Northwestern University Press, 1965), p. 327.

[2] Paul Ricoeur, "The Hermeneutics of Symbols and Philosophical Reflection," *International Philosophical Quarterly*, II, No. 2 (1963), 192–93.

evil can be discovered through a hermeneutic consideration of man's actual confession of evil.

That which ties the work of Ricoeur together is not any one of these themes, but their combination in his overall quest for a global philosophical anthropology. This search for an understanding of man is sufficiently comprehensive to include both finite and infinite, the voluntary and the involuntary, freedom and necessity, mind and body, abstract and concrete, perception and signification, symbol and reflection. The primordial image which illustrates best Ricoeur's entire phenomenological work is the vision of man as "situated," situated between the polarities of his reflective and active experience. A study of Ricoeur's thought brings this vision into realistic focus.

This central concern originally stimulated my interest in Ricoeur and, of course, it is central to this study. The problematic of this essay, the interrelation between mythic-symbolic language and the nature of man, is given form by this key issue in Ricoeur's thought. Ricoeur poses on answer to that problematic by demonstrating that a mythic-symbolic language is *necessary* for global understanding of man. But a consideration of mythic-symbolic language, not an early issue in Ricoeur's thought, occurs as a means of furthering the development of a philosophical anthropology, for it is by recourse to symbol and myth that the adventure of human freedom confronted by radical limitation is made explicit. In the original volume of *The Philosophy of the Will* the possibility for that development is latent, although the necessity for it emerges subsequently. I shall try to capture the dynamic movement of Ricoeur's thought by considering the "anthropological problematic" as it is centered in his earlier work and the emergence of mythic-symbolic language later. The first interpretive problem is methodological while the second concerns the development of a philosophical anthropology. In this chapter, I want to discover (1) what hermeneutics has to do with philosophy, and (2) how hermeneutics may be incorporated in an avowedly phenomenological philosophic program.

A. GLOBAL PHILOSOPHICAL ANTHROPOLOGY

No doubt every philosophical position has within it a certain model or image of an exemplary type which illustrates its aim and direction. Such a model may serve as a starting point which clarifies the later developments in such a way that it provides a key to give the interpreter of that position a fundamental sustaining insight into the direction of that orientation. The term global anthropology is taken most directly from *Fallible Man* the general concern of which is to further a discussion already begun in *Freedom and Nature* on the central human problem, the will. As a book, *Fallible Man*, attempts to make more concrete the reality of the basic internal rupture of the will revealed initially through the discussion of the relations of the voluntary and the involuntary processes of the will. It is out of this dichotomy that the global image emanates.

The problematic of *Fallible Man* consists in an attempt to find a way to reflect upon a double hypothesis: first, "that man is by nature fragile and liable to err," and second, that the "ratio" of fallibility comprises a "certain non-coincidence of man with himself." A moment ago it was indicated that Ricoeur depends primarily on the "Cartesian paradox of the finite-infinite man," the Platonic myth of misery, and Pascal's reflections on the dual nature of man for illumination. For Ricoeur, the central meaning of the three references is that they all conceive man as "situated" or "intermediate" between the diverse elements which make up his being.

Man is not intermediate because he is between angel and animal; he is intermediate within himself, within his selves.[3]

This self-perception by man himself is called a "pre-comprehension" to be conceived not as an ontological reflection, but as a foundation for reflection. Hence, the initial discussion is to be understood as an exercise in pre-philosophy which will establish a foundation for the actual philosophic elaboration of man's situational dilemma. At this point, the Platonic discourse on the soul is apt.

Unable to speak of it (the soul) in the language of Science, that is, in the discourse on immutable Being, the philosopher expresses it in the language of allegory, and then in the language of myth.[4]

Plato's concept of *thumos* designates dynamically the central human issue Ricoeur wishes to stress.

The soul appears as a field of forces undergoing the double attraction of reason called "that which urges" and of desire which is characterized as "something which holds back."[5]

---

[3] Paul Ricoeur, *Fallible Man*, trans. by Charles Kelbley (Chicago: Henry Regnery Co., 1965), p. 6.

[4] *Ibid.*, p. 13.

[5] *Ibid.*, p. 15.

In *thumos* one encounters a dangling man image wherein the suspended human subject "undergoes the double attraction of reason and desire." A correlate view is found in the Pascalian vision of the man who exists as a being intermediate between the very great and the very small, between infinity and nothingness, a man who is "a nothing in comparison with the infinite, and all in comparison with nothing." So Descartes, Plato, and Pascal have constructed a common view of man, suspended between a set of conflicting forces – a mixture.

Ordinarily the term "global" denotes a comprehensiveness that designates the unification of diverse elements which overcome the narrowness of perspectival views. On the level of modern moral investigation the dominant tendency has been to stress perspectival models, the major characteristic of which has been finitude. The global view conceived and developed by Ricoeur may be understood as something of a polemic against such perspectival views of man.

> By allowing ourselves to begin with the Cartesian theme of finite-infinite man – even though we may have to reinterpret it completely – we disassociate ourselves to some extent from the contemporary tendency to make finitude the global characteristic of human reality.[6]

But the term does not eliminate the situational perspectives that have been so predominant in contemporary investigations of the human dilemma. Rather the global notion attempts to present a more complex vision, hopefully a more adequate view of the matrix of human options that find their consequence in the evolution of contemporary radical limitation as a moral perspective. Hence a global view is something of a postulate, an hypothesis about the structure of human experience which presupposes a unity of that structure, but only as a possibility. To be suspended between a totality of options eliminates neither perfection nor limitation; rather it is the ontological characteristic which leads to the possibility of fallibility.

> Man's "ontological characteristic of being-intermediate consists precisely in that his act of existing is the very act of bringing about mediations between all the modalities and all levels of reality within him and outside of him."[7]

The global vision of man need not be a moral vision if the situational image is merely presented as a descriptive analysis of man without moral valuation. But the global view is preeminently moral because it allows for the possible emergence of the concept of fallibility. The situational view of man incorporates duality within totality in such a

---

[6] Ricoeur, *Fallible Man*, p. 6.
[7] *Ibid.*

way that suspension is between polar opposites. In themselves, neither duality nor polar opposition constitutes a moral perspective. Only when man is conceived as suspended between the most radical of the human polarities, the possibility of transcendence and the possibility of fault, does the global view become a moral view. The global view is conceived as a problematic vision because instead of presenting easy resolutions to the basic dichotomies of human experience, these dichotomies are revealed in such a way that their solution will be the critical issue which the philosophical system will attempt to resolve adequately.

The global view of the human dilemma is most directly the problematic in the book *Fallible Man*; indirectly the image appears elsewhere. For example, the problem of *Freedom and Nature* is to overcome an understanding of self and consciousness which fails to incorporate a realistic understanding of the role and function of the body involving the primary role of involuntary processes. In *The Symbolism of Evil* considerations of the extremes of the global view are given concretely through incorporation of the language of avowal (confession) in primary symbols and myths reincorporated through a hermeneutic method into philosophic discourse. In *De l'interprétation* an encounter with the works of Freud is undertaken to bring a more adequate (global) view of man into both psychological and philosophical discourse. The attempt to construct a global philosophical anthropology therefore will be understood as an originary starting point for the interpretation of Ricoeur's philosophical thought.

The process of thinking from the global image is a problem for the transformation of phenomenological methodology as well as for the substantial issue of this philosophical anthropology, namely the will with its correlate polarities, freedom and limitation. Under the rather broad rubric, phenomenology, Ricoeur has chosen to transform the phenomenological method from one grounded in classical Husserlian eidetics to one which finds hermeneutic interpretation as primary. No one methodology is sufficient to comprehend fully, describe adequately, and understand properly the multitude of issues to be included in a philosophical anthropology. With this method and its transformations, Ricoeur has attempted to struggle with the dialectic of freedom and limitation. Our approach will be to consider the methodological issues first, content issues second, and finally correlation of method and content in Ricoeur's later work.

1. *The Eidetic Method and Its Limitations*

Whatever Ricoeur's final judgment on the eidetic method, it sets the context for his original constructive work, *Freedom and Nature*. Classical phenomenology plays a central role in Ricoeur's thinking for he is concerned to retain his own version of Husserl's eidetic method, refusing to begin this constructive work on the basis of existential signification alone, as did many late post-Husserlian phenomenologists. The eidetic method which Husserl employed to constitute transcendentally acts of consciousness functions in a similar way for Ricoeur, although the primary datum is the willing subject cognizant and becoming cognizant of its activities. Therefore, the eidetic method functions at the most elemental level as a method of description which attempts to unfold the fundamental structures of voluntary and the involuntary under the rubric, will, as they are articulated in decision, bodily motion, and consent.[8] In this sense the description that the eidetic method undertakes is a "triadic interpretation of the act of the will,"[9] for "To say 'I will' means first, 'I decide,' secondly, 'I move my body,' thirdly, 'I consent.'"[10]

Eidetic, the adjectival derivation of *eidos*, Plato's alternative term for idea, was utilized originally in the phenomenological movement to designate essences. For Ricoeur, essence is too strong a term. The eidetic method describes, lays open, basic structures within a particular region; it is this function that distinguishes eidetic description from explanation. Explanation means "to move from the complex to the simple."[11] It is this orientation that dominates empirical psychology and the natural sciences. In contrast, the key term relating to description is "reciprocity," for here with the relation of the voluntary and the involuntary, the informing principle of each is the other. Ricoeur sees the relationship between the voluntary and the involuntary as the presentation of a reciprocity that transcends equality. The voluntary is always that which occurs as the primary and most immediate phenomenon. "I understand myself in the first place as he who says, 'I will.'"[12] It is this centrality of the willing self, what "the Stoic called the directing

---

[8] Paul Ricoeur, *Freedom and Nature: The Voluntary and the Involutary*, trans. by Erazim V. Kohak (Evanston: Northwestern University Press, 1966), p. 6.

[9] *Ibid.*

[10] *Ibid.*

[11] *Ibid.*, p. 4.

[12] *Ibid.*, p. 5.

principle"[13] that caused what Ricoeur believes to be the first Copernican revolution in philosophy.[14]

The striking characteristic of Ricoeur's version of the phenomenological method is his attempt to apply it to the area ordinarily thought to be most distant from the eidetic sphere of pure consciousness, namely the bodily involuntary. The basic assumption is that description is constituted by reciprocity so that the mutual interrelations of the voluntary and the involuntary will lead to understanding and intelligibility. The methodological benefit of descriptive orientation is that illumination is brought to the opaque and often incomprehensible realm of the involuntary by viewing it as reciprocal with the voluntary, while the voluntary, which is often conceived as in its non-complexity, is given richness through description in relation to the involuntary.

Ricoeur shares with classical phenomenology, and to a certain extent with the later or second generation phenomenologists, the use of the concept intentionality to recover and constitute the subjective world of meaning. Generally the more technical members of this group hold that ordinary uncritical perception and cognition is false, and that it is necessary to establish a reversal of attitudes involving a movement from a "natural attitude" to a phenomenological, or truly subjective attitude in order to discover the foundations of noetic meaning. Consequently consciousness is not associated with phenomenalism or sensationalism, but rather with intentional fields synthetically given to the realm of the subject.

Ricoeur's interpretation of intentionality is distinctive; while the difference between Ricoeur and Husserl is a subtle one.

Any function is constituted by its type of object, or as Husserl says, by its intentionality. We express it differently by saying that consciousness constitutes itself by the type of object to which it projects itself.[15]

The centrality of the notion "project" distinguishes Ricoeur's interpretation of intentionality from Husserl's because Husserl associated the notion with the reflective acts of pure consciousness instead of the dynamism of the will. From his, Ricoeur's point of view, the project is formulated in decision, becoming processively an action associated with bodily motivation, leading to complete formulation and execution. Viewed teleologically from its status as completed act, the project is defined as "acquiescence to necessity" because at that point the pro-

[13] Ricoeur, *Freedom and Nature*, p. 5.

[14] The term Copernican revolution is itself derived from Kant, who discovered that the self brings to perception certain aspects (a priori categories) which qualify perception.

[15] Ricoeur, *Freedom and Nature*, p. 6.

ject can no longer be changed. The notion of project could be designated as a simple volitional task, voluntarily initiated and voluntarily achieved. However, such a view cannot account for the complexities of voluntary-involuntary correlations and reciprocities. Rather, the involuntary side of bodily motivation presents "reasons" for voluntary action. The action (voluntary motion) which occurs as a consequence of a voluntary act (decision) reveals the involuntary organs of willing, habit, etc., that is, those things which make voluntary action possible but also place upon it its most radical limitation. Therefore, the range of volition incorporates necessity.

This doctrine of intentionality shares with traditional phenomenology the attempt to overcome a dualism between ordinary physical experience and psychological or mental experience. Ricoeur's argument bears within it Franz Brentano's original insight with regard to the distinction between genetic and descriptive psychology, an insight which, because of its focus on intentionality, was thought to be one of Husserl's most significant insights. Brentano wanted to find a fundamental characteristic which separates psychological perception and cognition from non-psychological ordinary perception and cognition of physical objects. The positivistic criticism of psychological experience had assumed that only those perceptions that could be tested were valid, perceptions of physical objects, whereas psychological experience, memories, judgments, dreams, etc. were untestable and therefore invalid. A sfar as Brentano was concerned the insight into the intentionality of psychic phenomena established their validity against the positivistic criticism inasmuch as psychic acts of consciousness retain an intentional relationship to an object. Consciousness is never empty. Consciousness is always intentional in the sense that it has reference to an object.

No hearing without something heard, no believing without something believed, no hoping without something hoped, no striving without something striven for, no joy without something we feel joyous about.[16]

Although Husserl was overwhelmed by Brentano's insight, calling it the key to phenomenological investigation, he went far beyond his onetime mentor by generalizing the notion of intentionality to apply to consciousness generally and universally. For Husserl all consciousness, not simply psychological perception, is intentional. Consequently, throughout his life Husserl sustained a polemic against empirical psycho-

---

[16] Herbert Spiegelberg, *The Phenomenological Movement* (2 vols. 2nd ed.; The Hague: Martinus Nijhoff, 1965), I, p. 39.

logy arguing that empirical psychology always grounded itself in an epistemologically uncertain physical model which reduced all perceptions to a physical scale. Ricoeur, sustaining this same phenomenological bias with regard to empirical psychology, finds the disturbing factor in such a psychology to be the "reduction of *acts* (with their intentionality and their reference to an Ego) to facts." Hence, the centrality of the human subject constituted in conscious acts is lost. But, the difference between Husserl and Ricoeur is worth noting. Ricoeur acknowledges the legitimacy of the so-called empirical disciplines finding that they have relevance to a phenomenological investigation because the knowledge obtained by such analysis may contribute to knowledge of the subject. Hence, the data derived from empirical disciplines may be reintegrated into a phenomenological context by a diagnostic method, essentially an eidetic analysis.

Ricoeur's interpretation of the eidetic method includes more than the repossession of consciousness to which Husserl directed the method; rather, Ricoeur seeks to enlarge the method to include consciousness of the body. To speak, therefore, of "becoming receptive to the Cogito's *complete* experience"[17] implies the extension of the eidetic method to include the involuntary structures, the bodily constitution of one's experience. This is a difficult task for the tendency of consciousness is to exclude bodily experience by dismissing it to be classified with the realm of objects. Ricoeur, not the first to find this insight into the splitting of the Cogito from itself in Descartes, finds the Cartesian genius in

having carried to the limit this intuition of a thought which returns to itself in positing itself and which takes into itself only an image of its body and an image of the other.[18]

In other words, consciousness tends to exclude consciousness of the body resulting in the conclusion that the "Cogito is broken up within itself."[19] Conscious reflection objectifies the body, an objectification which has led to treatment of the body in empirical psychology, biology, and the natural sciences generally as a natural object. Ricoeur, not wanting to reject the contributions of the natural and empirical sciences, wishes to make a transition from the objective view of the body to a subjective view wherein the involuntary can be understood in relationship to the voluntary and the Cogito can be restored to its rightful position.

[17] Ricoeur, *Freedom and Nature*, p. 8.
[18] *Ibid.*, p. 14.
[19] *Ibid.*

Such an enterprise is carried on in the name of freedom:

Freedom has no place among empirical objects; it requires a reversal of viewpoint and a discovery of the Cogito.[20]

This methodological process of freeing the body from empirical description where it appears as bound to a scheme of cause and effect, and
the process of recovering the true subjectivity of the body and relating it to the thinking self, has the consequence of restoring to the
Cogito that which is lost internally because of the splitting up of reflection and lost externally because of the treatment of the body as an
object. The Cogito, arrived at through an eidetics of the will, is complete in the establishment of a proper balance between freedom and
nature.

At the juncture of the phenomenological recovery of the body, that is,
the bringing back of the body into the realm of subjectivity, the eidetic
method is itself altered to meet the demands peculiar to bodily existence. The tendency of the self to posit itself (Descartes), and therefore to exclude bodily spontaneity is broken by what Ricoeur calls
"my incarnation as mystery." This means that the objectivity of description is deepened at each level of description by a movement towards a discovery of bodily spontaneity. "I need to pass from objectivity to existence." As the voluntary provides an opening for the discovery of the involuntary, so pure description of the structures of willing provides an opening for the recovery of bodily spontaneity. The
two motifs attempt to balance and overcome the possible dualism between the subjectivity of mental operations and the objectivity of
bodily descriptions.

If one should evaluate Ricoeur's usage and application of the eidetic
method against the backdrop of classical phenomenology, it is possible
to conclude that he has expanded that method to include bodily regions
often thought to be inaccessible to the methodologies of classical phenomenology. In another way however, Ricoeur places his own restrictive
limits on the method. A moment ago the claim was made that the
most radical form of Ricoeur's global philosophical anthropology occurs as the vision of man "situated" between the extremities, transcendence and fault. Surprisingly for Ricoeur, the eidetic method occurs not only as a means of internal bracketing of the structures of the
voluntary and the involuntary, but also as a means of excluding certain types of phenomena from the range of eidetic description. Transcendence and fault, so important for the overall understanding of

[20] Ricoeur, *Freedom and Nature*, p. 12.

Ricoeur's work, are excluded here. The process itself may be called one of double bracketing, suspending certain phenomena within brackets while excluding other phenomena which would appear ordinarily.

Ricoeur believes that if one begins the philosophical discussion with the immediate focus on fault and transcendence, the fundamental possibilities which can be illustrated by the eidetic method are thereby obscured

The greatest error we could make with respect to a fundamental ontology of willing and nature is to interpret it as an actual, immediate ethic.[21]

In order to avoid the possible obscurities that transcendence and fault would bring to a pure description of the will under the eidetic method, they are bracketed out momentarily only to be brought back in at a later point, in *The Philosophy of the Will*, Volume II, to be exact. Valuation of an ethical kind is excluded thereby on the ground that ethical pre-judgment, although ultimately necessary, is a mode of immediate falsification. The inclusion of fault simply will distract from an eidetic attempt to describe man's volitional nature in the sense that the Cogito's complete bodily experience, which it is the task of the eidetic method to clarify, is lost. Fault, with its correlates of radical evil and the rupture of the will, obscures the possible by illuminating the limitations of the actual. The full moral significance of the reconciliation between mind and body can be understood only after a neutral description of the voluntary and the involuntary is given. Finally, a total understanding of fault can be given on the basis of an analysis of myth and symbol, and that requires a hermeneutic method for elucidation, intelligibility and understanding.

But, if the eidetic method does not uphold the prospect for a global recognition of that ultimate "suspension" between transcendence and fault and the prospect for the ultimate reconciliation of these extremes in the human subject, it does sustain the possibility for another kind of reconciliation. Through opening up the realm of the body, through understanding thereby the unity of the voluntary willing self in reciprocity with the mysterious realm of the body, the eidetic method contains the possibility of sustaining and achieving on this abstract level the fundamental reconciliation of freedom and nature.

This study of the voluntary and the involuntary is a limited contribution to a far broader scheme which would be the reconciliation of a paradoxical and a reconciled ontology.[22]

[21] Ricoeur, *Freedom and Nature*, p. 22.
[22] *Ibid.*, p. 19.

In its broadest sense, the paradox is between freedom and nature in the context of an eidetic phenomenology.

There is no logical procedure by which nature could be derived from freedom (the involuntary from the voluntary) or freedom from nature.[23]

If, from an understanding of nature one could derive freedom, then the question of paradox would not arise. Yet, Ricoeur's contention is that the thematic term is reciprocity and paradox and not logical derivation. The actuality of paradox directs itself toward reconciliation, while the discovery of the reciprocity between freedom and nature will contribute toward that reconciliation. But a full concrete reconciliation is beyond the scope of the eidetic method.

One must conclude that Ricoeur's use of the eidetic method is based on the assumption that *an eidetics is necessary but not adequate.* The implicit necessity of an eidetic method is contained within each of the defining characteristics listed above. From the perspective of global philosophical anthropology each defining characteristic has its own implicit limitation. First, if the eidetic method can be applied to the development of the voluntary and the involuntary, it is necessary to go beyond the voluntary and the involuntary to deal adequately with the Cogito not only as perceived neutrally, but as experienced realistically. Second, to achieve this movement, it is necessary to break out of the brackets established originally to attain a neutral view of the basic structures of the will. Third, the very attempt to recover the complete experience of the Cogito requires that the eidetic method must be transcended so that the complete experience of the Cogito be related to the actual experience of the Cogito. Fourth, and perhaps most important, if the fundamental requirement of the eidetic method is that it is necessary to bracket out the actualities of transcendence and fault, and if as Ricoeur says, transcendence and fault are fundamental to an accurate elaboration of global anthropology, then it is necessary that the eidetic method must be dispensed with so that one can find a means for the reincorporation of transcendence and fault. Finally, if the ultimate direction of a global anthropology is toward the achievement of a full reconciliation of man with himself and the world, the eidetic method can suggest only the direction of such a movement; it cannot present the solution.

For all of these reasons it is in the name of an adequate global anthropology that the eidetic method is broken. The anthropological problematic is incorporated within the very structure of the eidetic

---

[23] Ricoeur, *Freedom and Nature*, p. 19.

method. Eidetics can present neutral structures, abstract possibilities. Eidetics cannot deal either with man who, as fallible, stands before the possibility of evil, nor can it appropriate fault as an actual immediate experience. *The introduction of a criterion of adequacy is itself the occasion for the demise of the eidetic method. It is this problematic that drives Ricoeur to a method of existential description.*

2. *Existential Description and Its Limits*

The debate among phenomenologists involves the relation of the eidetic (Husserl) to existential signification (Sartre, Heidegger). Perhaps there is no better testimony to Ricoeur's desire to bridge the various alternatives within the phenomenological movement, incorporating its best insights into his own thought, than his methodological movement from eidetic to existential description. One may conclude that neither eidetic nor existential description is adequate for a full global philosophical anthropology. Both are necessary for a full description. It is the *quest for adequacy* that gives to this mode of thinking its direction, drive and orientation.

Methodologically conceived, existential description requires a transition from the ideally possible to that which is possible in actuality. As Husserl thought of them, eidetic structures are to be associated with the ideal realm of pure possibility, and not connected with the radical limitations confronted by the human subject in his concrete day to day existence. As Ricoeur conceives of it, the transition from the realm of eidetic description to the realm of existential description may be understood as a transition from ideal to actual possibilities. This does not mean that one can transform the eidetic method into a kind of essentialism; rather a functional definition is intended. Eidetic description reveals functional possibilities. The eidetics of the will presents a distinct advantage over the empirics of the will in the sense that the eidetic method of bracketing can suspend structures, taking them out of their ordinary context, with the consequence that they are understood apart from the possible objectification that might occur in ordinary existential experience. In this sense the distinction between that which is possible ideally and that which is possible actually is immense. But no complete description of the human subject is possible without a movement from the ideal to the actual. Hence a transition must be made from that which is possible ideally to that which is possible actually in order to introduce those things which qualify man's actual experience, limiting thereby his fundamental possibilities to the realm of "concrete description."

So it is logical that existential description breaks the brackets in which the actuality of human fault was suspended originally. As we have seen, global philosophical anthropology understood on the most inclusive level is a philosophical anthropology which understands man as "situated" between transcendence and fault. Existential description provides a means to begin to reincorporate the realm of fault previously excluded. Fault was bracketed, Ricoeur suggests, because

fault...is not a feature of fundamental ontology similar to the factors discovered by pure description... Fault remains a foreign body in the eidetics of man.[24]

The inclusion of fault at the level of existential description poses a series of difficulties. Like eidetic description, existential description, fundamentally rational in orientation, is dominated by the motif of reflection upon acts of consciousness. Fault can begin to be reincorporated at this juncture on a conceptual level. The original brackets whereby fault was excluded, now discarded, do not allow for the complete presentation of fault and its correlate human evil in its full empirical actuality.

Existential description methodologically approaches not the full actuality of fault but fallibility as a possibility. The contention is that for evil and fault to be confronted in their full actuality it is necessary to deal with the concrete individual confessing his confrontation with evil. Such a confrontation requires another methodological revision, namely the transition to hermeneutics. So the methodological task of the work, *Fallible Man*, is to locate evil as a possibility within man through the application of a descriptive method which does not elucidate fault and evil per se, but the concept of fallibility. This is both the possibility and the limitation of existential description.

Under these carefully specified limitations of existential description the concept of fallibility can be approached in terms of a type of description which involves a transcendental, practical, and affective form of reflection. The prospect of fallibility is that finally it can locate the possibility of evil within man. The descriptive method in this existential form is able to derive the concept of fallibility by discovering through the knowing, acting, and affective aspects of the will, the confirmation of that original double hypothesis about the nature of man concerning his fragility and liability to err and his global dispropor-

[24] Ricoeur, *Fallible Man*, p. xvii.

tion with himself. The final meaning derived from existential description is "that the *possibility* of moral evil is inherent in man's constitution."[25] One may conclude: the function of existential description is to place global philosophical anthropology *before* the possibility of human fault and rupture.

Because the notion of fallibility has been introduced the transition from eidetic description to existential description provides the basis for the development of an ethic. As we have seen in *Freedom and Nature*, Ricoeur cautioned against the immediate plunge into an ethic claiming that the eidetic method with its neutral perspective and its necessary abstraction provides only the foundation for the latter possibility. The moral significance of the reconciliation between soul and body remained suspended requiring a long detour in order to be perceived.[26] This restriction disappears in *Fallible Man* and instead of offering caution, Ricoeur suggests that *Grandeur and Limitation of an Ethical Vision of the World* could have occurred as the "subtitle of this book." Ethical considerations are not limited to existential description, for it is by the method of hermeneutics that the actuality of freedom, evil and their interdependent relations are revealed. But existential description functions as the method which opens the door to ethics by preparing the way for the possibility of fallibility within the heart of man. This advance to ethical considerations is correlate with the movement toward the reinclusion of fallibility (*Fallible Man*) and the actuality of fault (*The Symbolism of Evil*). It is possible to conclude that simultaneous with the movement from eidetics to existential description is the movement from the abstract and neutral to the concrete and ethical.

As with eidetic description so with existential description, the limitations of method make necessary a further movement if a global philosophical anthropology under the rubric of the will can be attained. Each of the premises of the existential description orientation is not only an affirmation of the actual power and ability of that method; each has within it a fundamental limitation. If it is true that existential description requires a transition from the ideally possible to that which is possible in actuality, it is also true that existential description is limited, in fact, confined to the realm of evil as a possibility. It can only locate evil; it cannot fully probe its meaning. If it is true that existential description breaks the brackets in which the actuality of human fault was suspended, it is also true that existential description cannot fully

[25] Ricoeur, *Fallible Man*, p. 203.
[26] Ricoeur, *Freedom and Nature*, p. 22.

understand fault in its depth as that which is experienced and conferred as the source of evil. If existential methodology can only locate the fallible within man through a global description of the knowing, acting, and feeling subject, it cannot approach the consequences of that discovery. Finally, if existential description begins to work toward the foundation of an ethic, it is also the case that this method can only constitute a preliminary stage in that construction because it has only pointed to the source of evil as a possibility. It has not dealt with the concrete man who has committed an evil act. To overcome the limitations of existential description, it is necessary to turn to hermeneutics.

3. *Hermeneutic Phenomenology and Language*

Ricoeur contends that the limitation of a philosophical method which begins conceptually with fallibility is that it can confront fault only as a possibility. The case for hermeneutic phenomenology is sustained in the name of a desire to recover a direct experience of fault, for the question confronted is whether or not it is the lot of the philosopher to remain outside the actual experience of evil, condemned to the realm of purely possible considerations. Here we are at the boundary between existential description and the development of a hermeneutic. Either philosophy must remain within the realm of possibility or it must plunge into the slippery and opaque realm of statements about man's actual experience of evil. If philosophy confines itself to the realm of pure description, it can both locate the possibility of evil within man and it can show how man is liable to err simply because of the constitution of his being. Philosophy at that level can show that man is fallible; but it cannot deal with the fault that is the consequence of experienced fallibility. This is that "point of no return" where one questions whether or not philosophy can go beyond the realm of the immediacy of man's conscious experience. The advantage of remaining at this boundary is the advantage of clarity, that is, to remain in the realm of clarity, in the sphere of univocal concepts and meaning. But the "wager" results in the plunge into the realm of symbols and myth, the opaque realm of man's confession of evil. The problem is whether or not philosophy is capable of moving into this new milieu.

The term "wager" implies that there is a leap from fallibility to fault accounting for a movement into discourse on symbols and myths implying a movement from rational philosophical problems. This is deemed a wager because it is done on the assumption that the transition will enrich the discourse on freedom and limitation. Ricoeur makes the wager. He risks the possible loss of clarity for depth. He risks the loss of a clear but narrow vision of man for a global view of man. The hermeneutic occurs at this juncture not simply as an experiment in method but in the name of an attempt to recover the actual human experience of fault and the consequent quest for freedom. While fallibility is confined to the possible, it is in the name of this quest for the concrete that a hermeneutic phenomenology is established. In this sense, the wager marks the beginning of hermeneutics.

The realm in which the actual experience of evil is encapsulated is that confessional "language of avowal," a language the characteristics of which require a hermeneutic method of interpretation.

This language speaks for fault and evil to the philosopher, and what is noteworthy in it is that it is *symbolic* through and through.[27]

It is because the meaning of that language is hidden, opaque, and obscure that a new method is required to bring that language into the realm of philosophical reflection. The case for hermeneutic phenomenology then is predicated upon the assumption that the experience of evil can be encountered directly in a *particular* kind of language, that is, symbol and myth. Let it suffice to note here that the characteristics of that kind of language, to be considered later in detail, are to be distinguished from language which has as its aim and prerogative transparent conceptuality. At this point the methodological significance of this "turn to hermeneutics" requires consideration.

Ricoeur's argument with regard to this particular kind of language is not that it can be described by philosophy but that it actually functions as a pre-philosophical basis for philosophical reflection. Given the particular methodological context within which Ricoeur's thought is set, the departure is radical because it actually requires philosophy to give up temporarily reflection on the constitutive acts of consciousness (eidetic phenomenology) in order to turn to an explication of experience as it is given in pre-philosophical materials. Given this conception of the function of language, the constitutive foundation of philosophy is not to be found within the realm of philosophy at all but in that pre-philosophical language which provides the basis for philosophical reflection. It must be acknowledged consequently that the hermeneutic conception of phenomenology alters the Husserlian conception of philosophy in the sense that it departs radically from considerations of the constitution of the transcendental Cogito, to considerations of pre-

[27] Ricoeur, *Fallible Man*, p. xviii.

philosophical givens for later philosophical consideration and integration. As we shall attempt to show later, this does not mean a total departure from a phenomenological tradition, rather it means a transformation of phenomenology.

The key question raised by the use of symbols and myths, the language of avowal, is, if philosophy is required to turn to a pre-philosophical source for its fundamental data, how is it to bring that material back into the realm of philosophy? Ricoeur's reply is given in the hermeneutic thesis "the symbol invites thought." This is a distinctively non-reductionistic hypothesis with regard to the methodological analysis of symbolic language. Relying on the achievements of the phenomenology of religion, particularly those of Mircea Eliade, Ricoeur assumes that the status of the symbol in relationship to reflective analysis is one that construes the correlation between the symbolic form and philosophical reflection to be a non-positivistic one. Philosophy does not get behind the symbol with the explicit intention of eliminating that form; rather philosophy assumes that the symbol gives meaning. Mircea Eliade presented the case for the special function of the religious symbol well when he stated:

A religious phenomenon will only be recognized as such if it is grasped at its own level, that is to say, if it is studied as something religious. To try to grasp the essence of such a phenomenon by means of physiology, psychology, sociology, economics, linguistics, or any other study is false; it misses the one unique and irreducible element in it – the element of the sacred.[28]

Such a starting point, avowedly anti-reductionistic, allows the symbol to present its own meaning as a resource for philosophical reflection, while philosophical reflection attempts to bring that meaning into the realm of intelligibility, albeit not to exhaust the symbol but to understand it. It was then from the phenomenology of religion that Ricoeur derived an initial insight pertaining to the interpretation of symbols, namely, that the symbol must be interpreted on its own level with its own special set of rubrics and rules.

Methodologically speaking one is confronted with the problem of the construction of a theory of the symbol which attempts to define the symbol adequately while not submitting the symbol to a false reduction. In order to do this Ricoeur constructs a theory of symbol which distinguishes between the symbol and the sign making the contention that all symbols have a sign element within them while signs are not symbols. Signs find their primary identification in their one dimension-

[28] Mircea Eliade, *Patterns in Comparative Religion* (Cleveland: Meridian, 1963), p. xiii.

al conceptually clear identity being transparencies which strive for univocal meaning with singular intention. In contrast to the sign, the symbol is composed of polar dimensions to be identified not by univocity but by double intentionality. The significance of this notion of double intentionality is that in contrast to a conceptually clear language which is perhaps the aim of science, the language of the symbol is multivalent, designating in phenomenological terms, an intentional field of meaning.

The definition of the symbol as a doubly intentional phenomenon does not clarify the manner in which the intentionalities are presented, a problem most crucial to both the notions of the symbol and their later elaborations. The correlation between intentionalities settled upon by Ricoeur is this: that which constitutes the symbol has both a literal meaning and a symbolic meaning, the latter constituted by the former. Phenomenology of religion would suggest, for example, that the meaning of sky symbolism, sky gods, ascension symbolism, etc. always has a set of characteristics given by the sky, namely, the qualities of transcendence, infinity, eternality, etc. In this way the literal isness of the sky as an appearance is given through its various manifestations as sacred. In the context of *The Symbolism of Evil*, the symbol of stain may have an abstract, opaque reference to a feeling of psychic impurity, but this second intentionality is known through and constituted by a primary intentionality of stain which is the literal signification of stain, that is, a spot. Hence, the primary intentionality is that of literal signification, the spot, while the secondary intentionality of the symbol probes beyond the literal to manifest the feeling of psychic impurity which is derived from that primary form. It follows that the symbols of stain, sin, and guilt, the three basic symbols analyzed in *The Symbolism of Evil*, will find their methodological elaboration through the clues given by this intentional elaboration of the characteristics of symbols.

Ricoeur's theory of myth follows directly from this view of symbol. Myth is conceived as a secondary elaboration of symbolic material, in this context the application of a primitive hermeneutic to the primary symbols of stain, sin and guilt. The symbols of stain, sin and guilt find their original mythic context in the "myths of evil," a set of myths which composes two typological groups. The first group includes those myths which contain the drama of creation, the tragic myths in which the hero is subject to a fatal destiny, and myths of the soul in exile (the orphic myth). The second group of myths contains the "anthropological myth proper" which is defined by our author as the "biblical narrative of Adam's fall." As we shall discover in greater detail later, Ricoeur attempts to find the methodological solution to the correlation between the different typologies through a consideration of their content, evil. Essentially

the world of myth is ... polarized between two tendencies: one takes evil back beyond the human; the other concentrates it in an evil choice from which stems the pain of being man.[29]

The hermeneutic task then is to conceive these myths in a comparative way, discovering thereby the basic elements or structures within them which in turn illuminate the meaning of myth. A comparative or structural hermeneutic is employed to illuminate, in this case at least, the phenomenon at hand.[30] Again, Ricoeur has drawn heavily upon the phenomenology of religion to solve a primary hermeneutic problem, namely the task of moving from a set of data present but uninterpreted to the interpretation of that data. The basic problem of such a methodology is that understanding occurs through comparison. The symbols stain, sin, and guilt are placed beside one another in order to understand their mutual testimony to the fact of evil. In a similar way the myths are compared to uncover their meaning and their correlate structures. The conclusion of the analysis illustrates the double character of evil.

So again we come across, at a higher level of elaboration, the polarity of the primary symbols, stretched between a schema of exteriority, which is dominant in the magical conception of evil as stain, and a schema of interiority which only fully triumphs with the painful experience of the guilty and scrupulous conscience.[31]

In other words, evil illustrates two tendencies most clearly: the tendency to see evil as prior to man's experience of it, and the tendency to posit evil within man and make him the cause. It is the Adam myth, Ricoeur argues, which tends to include both aspects because it "has in fact two faces." In its most elemental form it is both the myth which asserts the priority of evil, like the symbol of stain, and yet it also locates evil within man as in the case of the symbol of guilt. From Ricoeur's perspective, the Adam myth is the anthropological myth proper because it is inclusive of the entire symbolism of evil.

Having elaborated briefly the theory of symbol and myth, it is

---

[29] Ricoeur, "The Hermeneutics of Symbols and Philosophical Reflection," 199.

[30] David Rasmussen, "Mircea Eliade: Structural Hermeneutics and Philosophy," *Philosophy Today*, XII, No. 2/4 (Summer 1968), 138–147.

[31] Ricoeur, "The Hermeneutics of Symbols and Philosophical Reflection," 199.

possible to develop Ricoeur's theory of hermeneutics based upon the proposition "the symbol invites thought." The invitation for hermeneutic reflection occurs on two levels, argues Ricoeur: the level of comparison and the level of wager. This movement may be considered circular inasmuch as thought from the symbol finally returns to its origin, namely the rediscovery of the symbol. The comparative level is the first level, that of bringing the various symbols and myths together and discovering their essential and structural relations. Ricoeur, however, wants to extend the hermeneutic method beyond the comparative level to include the question of truth which is suspended by the comparative method.

Symbols are given; they are also decided upon. There is a level beyond the comparative level wherein one has to make, on religious grounds at least, a decision for or against a particular set of symbols. Hence in contrast to the hermeneutic of the phenomenology of religions, Ricoeur extends his hermeneutic to include the problem of truth, that is, to the level of a truth which one can affirm. This notion of truth is associated closely with the concept of faith inasmuch as it is not given as an objective certainty but, as Pascal and Kierkegaard have shown, it is the correlate of a wager. At this point the hermeneutic circle includes personal involvement for "you must understand in order to believe, but you must believe in order to understand."

A hermeneutic procedure is informed by a choice, which instead of being the result of pure autonomy is associated with one's culture, tradition and history. Hence our author has chosen to opt for that tradition of thought on evil, both western and Christian, which is situated in that circular movement between faith and understanding. But the dialectic that has ensued in western thought between that which is understood and that which has been believed is at best a tenuous one. Ricoeur, aware of the rational demands of philosophic understanding on the one hand and the multivalence of symbolic forms on the other, tries to clarify the problem both historically and methodologically. In general philosophers attempt to use necessary and universal concepts to attain an understanding of reality. The symbol, however, presents a multiplicity of meaning; it is not universal and necessary in a univocal sense. Often, and this is the tragic story of the interpretation of symbols in the west, interpretation has meant demythologization in the sense that a false reduction of the symbolic form has been accomplished. So the process of philosophical reflection on symbols and myths is not an easy one. As we have seen, the two poles of the

symbolism of evil are the designation of evil as a matter of human responsibility and the feeling that evil is "already there," prior to one's
experience of it. Ricoeur finds that the history of reflection on the problem of evil has incorporated these two tendencies; inasmuch as it has
western thinkers have chosen either to allegorize or to gnosticize the
problem of evil. To allegorize is to rationalize, to divorce the literal
signification of the symbol from its symbolic signification. The gnostic
interpretation of the symbolism of evil has centered upon the experience
of evil as an experience prior to human responsibility making that interpretation into a kind of "dogmatic mythology." Consequently
the history of reflection upon evil tends to simplify the problem
making it either into a simple matter of human responsibility
or a matter of that which is prior to human responsibility. Of course
rationality and rational reflection has had little difficulty dealing with
the first option, for if evil is simply a matter of human responsibility,
then it is easily understood and quite resolvable, at least as a problem
on an abstract plane. But if one interjects the other side of the problem of evil, its priority to human experience, it becomes absurd, something which reason cannot fathom. So reason and reflection can
account for evil as a matter of human responsibility, but thought
reaches a limit when evil is experienced as tragically present. This is of
course a dilemma, in many ways a hermeneutic dilemma. But perhaps it illustrates the significance of a hermeneutic investigation with
its circular dialectic, radically inclusive of both that which is easily
accessible to reflection and the point at which reflection reaches its
limit. When one understands evil as something that transcends one's
personal acts, then evil exists as something that precedes man. The
consequence of this insight is a return to the tragic which defies ration-
alization. At this point the hermeneutic circle is complete. Thought
reaches its limit and it must return to the symbol.

   We are now in a position to probe the question of the contribution of
hermeneutics from the perspective of phenomenological method. What
does phenomenological hermeneutics contribute to philosophical reflection that is not already given in eidetic and existential description?
Here we touch again upon the perilous question of the proper interpretation of symbols without their destruction, that is, an interpretation
that avoids gnosis and allegory.

   The symbol gives a richness and consciousness to that which has
otherwise had an abstract character. To confront the experience of
fault on the level of its immediate confessional utterance in all its

variety in symbols and myths is to introduce a symbolic richness to reflection that would be otherwise unattainable. The question remains what is actually and specifically contributed to thinking by this orientation?

"The riddle of the slave-will (to be discussed in another context in the following chapter), that is, of a *free will which is bound and always finds itself bound*, is the ultimate theme that the symbol gives to thought."[32] On the one hand, this is what the symbol and the myth signify, which is another way of stating that evil is understood in terms of freedom. Although Ricoeur wishes to avoid the possibility of gnosis and allegory, he realizes that philosophy temporarily falls into this trap with the ultimate hope of returning to the symbol. Reflection itself is a form of "demythologizing"[33] and its risk is allegory, that is, to break the symbolic aspect of the symbol from its literal ground.

Reflective thought is essentially demythologizing, it interprets mythology by reducing it to allegory. The problem of evil is in this regard an exemplar: *reflection upon the symbolism of evil reaches its peak in what we shall call the vision of evil*.[34]

It is significant that Ricoeur finds Augustine to be one who first elaborated this allegorical interpretation of evil most fully in his protest against the Manichaean doctrine of evil. Augustine attempted to show that evil was its own cause; he saw evil at the heart of freedom and therefore not derived from a source or cause outside man. For Ricoeur it is Kant who carries this reflection to a place of utmost clarity by showing that freedom itself is the power of deviation,[35] a form of subversion. If reflection, by its departure from the symbol, can show that evil lurks at the very heart of freedom and has no other cause than freedom, one has reached a point of utmost clarity but at the price of depth. What is lost by this departure from the symbolism of evil is the other side of evil, its tragic aspect.

The tragic aspect of evil first expresses itself in the literal character of stain, the spot, something already there, prior to the exercise of freedom, "evil as tradition."[36] It is this side that allows for the gnostic interpretation of evil, the temptation to put evil in a framework, to express it independently of freedom. Again Ricoeur calls upon Augustine and Kant. The expression of this theme par excellence is the Pau-

---

[32] Ricoeur, *Fallible Man*, p. xxiii.
[33] Ricoeur, "The Hermeneutics of Symbols and Philosophical Reflection," 204.
[34] *Ibid.*
[35] *Ibid.*, p. 208.
[36] *Ibid.*, 209.

line-Augustine interpretation which places guilt *in Adam*; therefore evil is understood to be prior to each individual existence. Augustine tried to work this out in the Pelagian controversy by relying on themes of reprobation and of biological generation. Intellectually, Augustine found evil prior to man and then made him responsible for it. In terms of logic and clarity, Pelagius was essentially right in the perspective of his argument. But for Ricoeur Pelagius is the perfect example of clarity without depth. Although Pelagius was right intellectually, Augustine was right experientially when he turned to the "pseudo-concept of original sin."[37] For Kant this view was developed in terms of his notion of a priori, that is, the a priori possibility of evil as ground of actual evil. Ricoeur finds Kant complementary to Augustine since he alleviated most of the "dogmatic mythology" from this side of evil by simply showing its a priori condition as possibility.

To what conclusion can the reflection following the symbol come? On the one hand it can elaborate evil as contingent, at the heart of freedom, present in every free act. On the other, it can see evil as necessary, prior to every individual act, ethical in the former sense, tragic in the latter. But that is the problem, is there any rational way to include both the necessity and the contingency of evil in a single reflection? Ricoeur's answer is that every attempt to include the "totality" has failed.

For either the thought of necessity leaves contingency aside, or it so includes it that it entirely eliminated the "leap" of evil which posits itself and the "tragic" of evil which always precedes itself.[38]

It either takes the gnostic (dogmatic mythology) or the allegorical path opting for clarity at the loss of depth. We reach the point where reflection is driven to its limit. There is no purely rational way of synthesizing the contingency and necessity of evil and this is precisely the point where the hermeneutic circle is completed, for reflective thought is driven back to the symbol because the symbol can retain this multivalence while reflective thought cannot. Reflective thought is driven back to evil in two ways. First, understanding has reached its limit and one is driven back to faith. The symbol is simply reaffirmed. Second, the return to symbolism is motivated by an attempt to recover in symbols a reconciliation, a renewal of thought that has reached its limit in symbols of evil.

It remains to evaluate both the claims and the consequences of a

---

[37] Ricoeur, "The Hermeneutics of Symbols and Philosophical Reflection." 211.
[38] *Ibid.*, 215.

phenomenological hermeneutic. The argument for turning philosophy toward the language of avowal was sustained on the assumption that through a confrontation with this language of symbol and myth it would be possible to confront concretely the experience of fault which had heretofore remained an abstraction, a possibility.

It seems that hermeneutic phenomenology based upon the language of avowal contributes to the elaboration of global anthropology in the following ways. Hermeneutic phenomenology, given the pre-established basis and orientation of Ricoeur's thought, may be understood to advance the quest for global anthropology by finding in language a *concrete ground* for fault, the disturbing problem and central issue of the global view of man. The question is, is this a more adequate way of reflecting on man than the reflection under the previous methodologies? The case for hermeneutics providing a more adequate mode for reflection can be established by Ricoeur in two ways: Internally, the drive in Ricoeur's thought is directed toward man's concrete and elemental experience. Thought from the symbol has a concrete basis. It is grounded in an actual experience of evil and it does not go beyond that actual experience. The methodological concern for adequacy is complimented by the development of a hermeneutic. On the external side, that is, the relation of hermeneutics to other possibilities, it is possible to indicate the options that Ricoeur wishes to dismiss. Not only does symbol provide a concrete ground for global anthropology, it is in fact *a guide*. The symbol invites thought; it shapes the character of hermeneutics but it also functions as a guide to thought. Not only does the symbol stimulate thought, it also provides a criterion for reflection. The gnostic and allegorical alternatives are cases in point. The attempt to place evil in the context of either a reflective or an ethical system wherein the symbolic dimension is lost is itself to be resisted. Ricoeur is adamant in his desire not to make evil into a principle of negativity nor to give it the status of pure *necessity*.

Thus, thought from the symbol is judged by the symbol. Thought which moves from the symbol can contribute to global anthropology by itself providing a *limit* for reflection. The symbolism of evil is instructive in this regard, for the confession that evil precedes man and is therefore prior to freedom provides a hiatus which cannot be bridged by reflection. The interruption of reflection drives one back to the symbol wherein the original faith stance in affirmed. Consequently, the dominant realism of this hermeneutic position may be affirmed over speculative idealism or journalistic moralism. Ricoeur's thought does not reduce an understanding of man to a narrowness which sacrifices depth for clarity. The hermeneutic method contributes to that end. The advantage of this perspective is that accomplished by seeking a philosophical resource in a particular kind of language. Ricoeur's hermeneutics is not derived *de novo*, but is in fact the result of his confrontation with the issues of phenomenological methodology, that is, the advantages and limitations of eidetics, the methodological problems of man's actual experience of evil and issues of language. Any adequate interpretation of Ricoeur's hermeneutic position requires a consideration of the total methodological struggle and accomplishment that dominates his thought. Further, in achieving the first aspect of the correlation which is the subject matter of this discussion, it has been necessary to go back to the original considerations of methodology in Ricoeur's constructive work. It is assumed that the same must be done in considering Ricoeur's philosophical anthropology.

III

FREEDOM AND GLOBAL ANTHROPOLOGY

Whatever methodological title one gives to Ricoeur's major work, it is basically a treatise on the philosophy of the will. It should not be regarded as unusual therefore if one discovers within that discussion a phenomenological treatment of the traditional themes which have dominated discussion of the will since Saint Paul, and from the perspective of *The Symbolism of Evil*, before that time in terms of the central role of those themes, particularly in western religious symbolism and mythology. There is a dialectical interplay of freedom and bondage, ideal possibility and actual limitation, fault and transcendence, freedom and evil, which create the foundation for the development of the basic themes. The fact that traditional themes predominate does not mean that Ricoeur's discussion and presentation of the philosophy of the will is in any sense a traditional presentation. Ricoeur has attempted to bring that discussion into the context of the phenomenological method by specifying man's fundamental possibilities under the rubric of the "will" primarily through the eidetic delineation of the structures of voluntary and involuntary, the existential specification of fallibility, and the hermeneutic elaboration of actual fault. The reason for Ricoeur's choice of the subject "will" reveals his ties with contemporary French phenomenology.

It was Husserl who attempted to establish a philosophical foundation through the elaboration of a phenomenological method fundamentally epistemological in character. It was Sartre[1] who changed that method from one of contemplation to one of action. Originally the phenomenological method under Husserl was one that sought to recover the foundations of thought. Husserl wanted to recover the primary acts of consciousness through the eidetic reduction and descrip-

[1] Jean-Paul Sartre, *Being and Nothingness* (New York: Washington Square Press, Inc., 1966).

tion, thereby revealing their intentional mode. Heidegger tried to press this quest for foundations by attempting to get behind these fundamental acts of consciousness in order to establish their ontological foundation. Sartre accepted this basic distinction given by Heidegger between acts of consciousness and immersion in being which Heidegger argued made them possible. Sartre went on to make a Hegelian distinction between being-in-itself and being-for-itself, and therefore consciousness arose as it negated itself from being-in-itself, thus becoming itself by a nihilistic act, resulting in the cleavage between the being which is "in-itself" and the nothingness which is the becoming of consciousness. The distinction between Sartre and Husserl at this point is, that for Husserl, conciousness is fundamentally noetic and contemplative, while for Sartre, consciousness is active – the consciousness makes itself. The fundamental problem for man from this perspective is freedom. For consciousness to become what it is, it is necessary that it free itself from its objectification in being-in-itself in order to become being-for-itself.

By focusing upon the problem of man's will, making human freedom the central issue of his thought, Ricoeur stands at the center of this phenomenological discussion. In this sense, like Sartre, he has chosen to deal with consciousness in this fundamentally active mode, and it is possibly this revision he accepts. But if freedom is man's central problem, it is precisely at this juncture that Ricoeur disagrees with Sartre. Ricoeur has wanted to develop a doctrine of the will which understands freedom in the context of nature rather than as a rejection of it. Therefore he has chosen, in his elaboration of the will, to follow Merleau-Ponty's desire to base this phenomenology of perception on the pre-reflexive basis of the world. It is not in negation that the will realizes itself, but in its incorporation of the involuntary, the world, and nature. Like Merleau-Ponty's thesis that perception occurs in the midst of the world, Ricoeur finds a freedom in the midst of nature, the pre-reflexive foundation of phenomenological reflection is the world, the body, or the involuntary.[2] It is from this juncture that freedom moves. When Thévenaz commented on Sartre and Merleau-Ponty he could well have included Ricoeur in his statement. He said Sartre's

thought is oriented, like that of Merleau-Ponty, towards the analysis of engagement, action and history. The French phenomenologists who are the philoso-

[2] M. Merleau-Ponty, *Phenomenology of Perception* (London: Routledge and Kegan Paul. 1962).

phers of the "Resistance," brutally thrown into history and encamped before Marxism, cannot dodge these questions.[3]

It is not unusual that Ricoeur should have chosen the will as the subject for philosophic interpretation.

In both the technical area of consciousness and reflection specified by the phenomenological method, and in the general area of practical engagement in issues of action and ethics, the choice of the will and the issues of freedom present themselves as the central and absorbing theme of his basic enterprise. The context for this theme is a global view of man. As we have seen, this subject is given specification through the eidetic, existential and hermeneutic modes of reflection.

The centrality of the issue of freedom in Ricoeur's philosophy of the will suggests three guidelines for interpretation: freedom and nature, freedom and fallibility, and freedom and fault. To so centralize the interpretation of man on the problem of freedom is not, in this instance, a reductive enterprise because Ricoeur's notion of freedom is one that in contrast to Sartre's negation is affirmative, and at the same time it attempts to be inclusive. Thus Ricoeur's argument is that an adequate understanding of freedom can be described only as a freedom which is informed by nature, a freedom which realistically considers the possibility of fallibility, a freedom in confrontation with the actuality of fault.

In terms of the overall context of this discussion freedom is the substance of a global anthropology since the consequence is that freedom is ultimately the correlate of mythic-symbolic language. Freedom and its limit constitute the anthropological ground of mythic-symbolic language for if mythic-symbolic language and philosophical anthropology are correlated ultimately in Ricoeur's thought, that correlation will depend upon the function of freedom. Consequently, in order to understand the role of freedom and its limit in relation to symbols and myths, it is necessary to conceive the anthropology of freedom and limit in the entirety of Ricoeur's constructive work.[4]

---

[3] Pierre Thévenaz, *What is Phenomenology?* ed. by James M. Edie (Chicago: Quadrangle Books, Inc., 1962), pp. 82–83.

[4] The central theme of Ricoeur's thought, from the point of view of his attempt to construct a philosophical anthropology, is freedom and its limitations. Although Ricoeur originally considered freedom in relationship to nature, later he turned to myth and symbol as phenomena constitutive for the experience of freedom and its limitation.

A. FREEDOM AND NATURE

Ricoeur's original doctrine of freedom, conceived and developed in the context of his first constructive work, Volume I of *The Philosophy of the Will*, is neither a freedom from anxiety in the Kierkegaardian sense, nor a freedom from negation in the Sartrian sense. It is not supported by the elaboration of cosmology as in Hegel. The doctrine of freedom that is presented by Ricoeur can be understood as no ordinary treatise on the freedom or the related bondage of the will in the Augustinian or the Lutheran sense. It is Ricoeur's intention to exclude from discussion at the outset, the problem of bondage to "passions and the law."[5] The original understanding of freedom given in Ricoeur's thought is one which under the clarity of the eidetic method locates the will in the context of voluntary and involuntary processes. Ricoeur is concerned not to present an abstract doctrine of freedom but one which begins in relation, not freedom independent of nature but dependent upon and united with nature. His fundamental methodological principle is the reciprocity of the voluntary and the involuntary. Each functions for the other with the consequent conclusion that the voluntary is neither ruled by nor separated from the involuntary inasmuch as Ricoeur's thesis is that the involuntary (bodily spontaneity, habits, spontaneous reflexes, needs, emotions, etc.) provides the basis for any possible voluntary activity. The involuntary is both the possibility for and the limit of freedom because freedom is only real in relationship to the involuntary, the reference of which is to the body. By attempting a reconciliation with the body, Ricoeur is fulfilling the attempt (cited earlier) to achieve a repossession of the *Cogito* and to achieve a reconciliation of the *Cogito*. He regards this task as a solution to the mind-body dualism and a fulfillment of the original program elaborated by Marcel in terms of the recovery of the meaning of the body as incarnation.

Ricoeur's original discussion of the will is organized under an act of the will containing three voluntary movements: I decide, I move my body, I consent – voluntary movements sustained by the act of the will. In each separate instance the voluntary movement involves a correlate involuntary inasmuch as the involuntary provides "reasons" for the voluntary, while the voluntary provides a focus upon the invol-

---

[5] Paul Ricoeur, *Freedom and Nature: The Voluntary and the Involuntary*, trans. by Erazim V. Kohak (Evanston: Northwestern University Press, 1966), pp. 20–22.

untary. It is necessary to consider these three moments in the process of willing in order to understand Ricoeur's original doctrine of freedom in the context of the will.

1. *Freedom and Decision*

The will analyzed under the method of pure description reveals a decision because intentional analysis discloses that

A decision signifies, that is, designates in general a future action which depends on me and which is in my power.[6]

Intentionality of decision simply designates a project for future action, but with the added stipulation that it invokes, or better imputes the self as the pre-reflexive basis for that decision in such a way that any attempt to deal with a pure consciousness apart from this personal imputation is initially fallacious. Instead of the naturalistic explanations of decision in the light of causality, Ricoeur associates decision with motive, refusing a definition which would make motive into a cause which is separate from the decision. He is concerned to avoid a purely ethical definition of motivation which associates the process of decision immediately with an interpretive scheme, obscuring the actual structure of decision. Decision, seen from the perspective of the subject (self-imputation) associated with motivation, provides the appropriate context for the interpretation rather than the imposition of a causal physics or an immediate ethic. The argument is that from this perspective one may describe "the bond of activity and reciprocity (which) indicates the fundamental limit of a freedom which is that of a man's will rather than the will of a Creator."[7]

The intentional analysis of decision, which opens up the region of the involuntary as a source of motivation for decision, applies the methodological principle "The involuntary is *for* the will and the will is *by reason* of the involuntary."[8] In terms of the analysis of decision, once having placed decision under intentional analysis in the sphere of the voluntary, it is possible to probe beneath the voluntary to discover the manner in which the corporeal involuntary provides the foundation for voluntary action. This approach has the advantage of achieving an understanding of the voluntary which is informed by the involuntary in the sense that the involuntary exists for the will. Consequently, the

---

[6] Ricoeur, *Freedom and Nature*, p. 43.
[7] *Ibid.*, p. 84.
[8] *Ibid.*, p. 86.

body, rescued from the false reductions of empirical observations which conceive the body as object, is perceived as an aspect of a living subject.

The involuntary correlate of voluntary decision as project, understood on the voluntary level as empty designation, is defined as need. All those things which motivate the body to act without any pre-conceived consciousness of this action, the desire for food, sleep, etc., are associated with need. Ricoeur conceives the interrelation of need and imagination in desire to be the foundation of the reciprocal relationship between the voluntary and the involuntary because need, as the bodily experience of that which is lacking, becomes an object requiring an act of the will for its fulfillment. In this primordial reciprocity of the voluntary and the involuntary value is introduced inasmuch as pleasure, the object of need entertained by desire, is valued as good while pain is valued as evil. In the latter case however, the process is only similar because pain has its source in fear and not in need. Yet Ricoeur's point is that when the corporeal involuntary is incorporated into the methical consideration of value a more complete description is attained thereby.

Within this analysis we see once again Ricoeur's attempt to expand the restrictive areas of the classical eidetic method to include the bodily involuntary as part of the constitutive world of experience and meaning. The analysis of choice which is included within the description of decision is then one which attempts to get beyond a simple voluntarism by considering those factors which embody choice in the incarnate involuntary. An inclusive view of choice therefore attempts to overcome the false dichotomies between the irrational and the rational, the anti-intellectual and the intellectual by including that which is excluded by other methodologies. Hence, Ricoeur's claim is that decision has a history, from hesitation to choice, inclusive of bodily motivation which informs the process. Whereas hesitation is like the empty designation of decision and need, choice depends upon motivation. But inasmuch as choice is dependent upon the body, the motivation of choice is initially undetermined because the multiplicity of motives presented to it yields to no distinctive order. In other words, choice moves slowly from a consideration of bodily indetermination to the discovery of a resolution which is both continuous and discontinuous with the original project of the will in the sense that choice can be read as a breaking off from that which has gone before its completion.

A beginning definition of freedom is freedom informed not only by purely rational and voluntary considerations but also by pre-rational and involuntary explanation. By bringing these seemingly contrary aspects of experience together this position begins to sketch a definition of freedom which attempts to derive a non-cosmological view in this sense: Ricoeur has followed Husserl's cue with regard to the phenomenological reassessment of traditional dualisms between mental freedom and objective necessity. Husserl believed a new metaphysics and a new ontology could be derived from a phenomenological methodology for once having left the realm of the natural attitude one dicovered that inherited dualisms of ordinary experience were false ones. Once an eidetic reduction was performed it was clear that all experience was constituted consistently by a transcendental subject. Although the notion of freedom is at this point somewhat sketchy, it is clear that Ricoeur, working under an expanded view of the eidetic method has attempted to include the exploration of bodily regions, that old realm of material necessity, without falling into the trap of constructing a cosmology that supports dualism. Hence, from the perspective of the first moment of an act of the will, the act of decision, a doctrine of freedom is presented which can be contrasted with a cosmological definition of freedom.

The ultimate consequence of the Cartesian revolution seems to us to lie here, in the discovery that the originality of consciousness with respect to all objectively conceived freedom is such that no cosmology can any longer engulf this consciousness.[9]

2. Freedom and Action

Decision must be considered in the first moment as an act of the will because decision initiates the activity of the will marking its beginning. Decision is a kind of designation, empty without that which contributes to its fulfillment. Intentional analysis of an act of the will reveals that second moment of voluntary motion or action when decision is acted upon which moves the process of deciding towards its conclusion. Voluntary motion, the simple "I move my body," brings the movement of the will from the intentional ideal to the practicality of action. From the perspective of the intentionality of action, acting is a "presence,"[10] yet something accomplished by the self, while practically the intentionality of acting is a "way in which a subject relates himself to

[9] Ricoeur, *Freedom and Nature*, p. 191.
[10] *Ibid.*, p. 205.

objects."[11] Action perceived in relationship to its object allows Ricoeur
to introduce the notion of pragma which he defines as the "correlate
of doing."[12]

Thus far Ricoeur conceives action as an intention plus its object, the
intention being directed toward its object, the pragma. Between these
two points, in the scheme of action Ricoeur places the body: *"the body
is not the object of action but its organ."*[13] As in the case of decision, the
body is implicated in the process of moving from the intentionality of a
phenomenon of the will to its completion.

Here phenomenological description confronts the major difficulty
of attempting to overcome problems of dualism posited originally between that which appears to consciousness and that which occurs to
empirical observation, that is, the hiatus between mental and physical
facts. The introduction of the body into a study of voluntary motion
presents the problem of overcoming a dualism of the voluntary and
involuntary. Ricoeur accepts the challenge presented to an adequate
description of the will. "Phenomenology must go beyond an eidetic
which is all too clear, and go on to elaborate the 'indices' of the mystery
of incarnation."[14] The task is to move beyond the original epistemological dualism to repossess the true relation of the voluntary and the
involuntary at the level of the context of action and therefore achieve a
full understanding of the *Cogita*.

Ricoeur, not content to reject the findings of scientific interpretation
as irrelevant to the investigation of the phenomenology of the will,
chooses to apply a diagnostic interpretation to those findings which
complement understanding of the reciprocity of the voluntary and the
involuntary at the level of action (that is, an interpretation which frees
the data primarily of gestalt psychology and other sciences from ob-
jectivistic description). Informed by the achievements of intentional
analysis and diagnostically interpreted scientific analysis, one is able
to turn to the involuntary as the informant of voluntary action. There
are three primary areas of involuntary motion which require consideration under the rubric of action: performed skills, motion, and habit.
The former are allied closely to the objective scientific notion of reflex. Yet Ricoeur wishes to make a distinction between the performed
skill and the reflex, holding that the performed skill is a "primitive

---

[11] Ricoeur, *Freedom and Nature*, p. 208.
[12] *Ibid.*, p. 210.
[13] *Ibid.*, p. 212. (Italics in text).
[14] *Ibid.*, p. 219.

pattern of behavior of our body in relation to perceived objects."[15] The reflex is defined as a form of "elementary adaptation"[16] which from this phenomenological point of view is to be understood in relation to the performed skill. The distinction Ricoeur wishes to make is clarified in his discussion of defense and protection, not primarily as a reflex but as a performed skill. To be sure, there is a reflexive reaction to pain. The performed skill differs from the reflex in that the individual is able either to anticipate or sustain the "courage of acting in spite of pain which must be undergone."[17]

The theme under which the performed skill occurs is Maine de Brian's *Homo Simplex in Vitalitate*.[18] In the performed skill as related to action one is able to uncover the fundamental unity of the voluntary and the involuntary, not only in relation to defense but also in relation to appropriation, exploration, and accommodation. Whereas reflex can inform that process, it tends to receive isolated consideration.

One aspect of bodily spontaneity contributing to action is performed skills; a second is emotion. Ricoeur's analysis of emotion designates three types of emotion as primary: the emotion of wonder, shock, and passion. For Ricoeur, like Descartes, the emotion of wonder is the most elemental, a kind of primordial unifying emotion which supports an initial unity of bodily and voluntary impulses. Shock is often understood as disruptive and for that matter, particularly in extreme cases of fear and pain, shock potentially incapacitates the will and thereby leads to disunity. While the emotion of wonder in its most concrete form as desire "brings together all the involuntary within the confines of the act,"[19] emotions of shock may lead to a general incapacity of the voluntary. The emotion of passion differs from wonder and shock and in many ways is the most difficult to specify. "Passion is consciousness which binds itself."[20]

Habit is the third realm of bodily spontaneity which informs voluntary motion and action. Habit, like performed skills and emotions, is something which is situated primarily in the realm of the involuntary but which presents indices to the unity of the voluntary and the involuntary on the level of bodily spontaneity. Habit is distinguished from the other two by its dependence upon learning. A habit is ac-

---

15 Ricoeur, *Freedom and Nature*, p. 232.
16 *Ibid.*, p. 235.
17 *Ibid.*, p. 237.
18 *Ibid.*, p. 249.
19 *Ibid.*, p. 266.
20 *Ibid.*, p. 277.

quired[21] and through the process of acquisition becomes a second nature in the sense that it allows the self to perform skills that it would otherwise be incapable of. Habit may therefore be defined as the "useful naturalization of consciousness,[22] a reversion from freedom, the habit acquired by will applied to nature, the realm of the involuntary.[23]

For Ricoeur the resolution of bodily spontaneity in terms of the role of the will occurs by description of the function of effort. Decision, seen in relation to involuntary structures, was resolved by accommodation of choice. Voluntary motion, the "I move my body," becomes real through a consideration of the function of muscular effort as it gives unity to the multiple possibilities presented by the body. It is possible to conceive a correlation between the will and ability that would see effort in perfect harmony with bodily ability. In actuality this possible harmony is replaced by a bodily docility which presents to the will the problem of overcoming and ordering bodily spontaneity.

Consequently the dialogue at this juncture, ultimately a dialogue of freedom and nature, of the voluntary and the involuntary, is one involving bodily ability and willing. It is just this fact, namely that a dialogue can be established at all, that is important at this point. Rather than placing reflexive action in the realm of reductionism to stimulus-response theories which eliminate consciousness on the basis of objective models, the human subject is here considered in relationship to reflexive action so that freedom is informed by such activity. Hence, to follow the argument as it has developed thus far, Ricoeur has attempted, with considerable consistency, a dual critique in this dialogue of the voluntary and the involuntary. By the use of a diagnostic method he has attempted to bring within the realm of phenomenological analysis materials heretofore considered under the rubric of a purely objective consideration, or as Husserl would say, materials subject to the naiveté of the natural attitude. Hence, while not rejecting materials of the so-called sciences he has brought them into a phenomenological context. Second, by so doing he has attempted a reconciliation between the dualisms of mind and body present in classical cosmology. However, the most radical statement of the problem and its solution is yet to be presented in the consideration of freedom and consent.

---

[21] Ricoeur, *Freedom and Nature*, p. 282.
[22] *Ibid.*, p. 307.
[23] *Ibid.*, p. 286.

3. *Freedom and Consent*

A complete act of the will is not simply decision, nor is it only action; the final moment in the three-fold act of the will is consent. Once a decision has been made, and once an action has been embarked upon, necessity becomes the fact to which the will must consent. Consequently, there is an inevitability in the final end result of the willing process. Of the three movements, consent is the most crucial to the willing process because consent brings into focus the difficult problem of the relationship between *freedom and necessity*. "Now we can fathom what is at stake in consent: it is the ultimate reconciliation of freedom and nature which both theoretically and practically appear to us torn apart."[14]

To deal with the problem of consent is no slight task, given the general dichotomy between freedom and necessity sustained by modern existentialism. Kierkegaard inaugurated the dilemma by posing an absolute dichotomy between freedom and necessity. He suggested that man's problem was one of being tied to his worldly existence. The project of Kierkegaardian existentialism was to free man from his ties to the world in order that he might realize the possibilities of his own existence. It remained for Sartre to re-emphasize this radical cleavage between freedom and necessity by making the distinction between being-in-itself (necessity) and being-for-itself (freedom). Ricoeur, with his concern to overcome the epistemological dualism of Descartes and with his desire to incorporate the body incarnate (Marcel), sees the issue not as the radical dichotomy of freedom and necessity but as the possibility of reconciliation. The problem then is to see that "Consent is the movement of freedom towards nature in order to become reunited with its necessity and convert it into itself."[25] The problem of consent is affirmation. How does freedom take necessity into itself without annihilation"? Two difficulties present themselves. From a psychological perspective it seems that the final resolution of freedom and necessity in consent is determinism. From a philosophical perspective does not the involuntary triumph over the voluntary? The problem of consent is to specify the bodily (involuntary) areas of consent and to show how they are affirmed by the voluntary (freedom).

Ricoeur believes that consent, from an involuntary perspective, can be probed from three basic areas: character, consciousness, and life.

[24] Ricoeur, *Freedom and Nature*, p. 436.
[25] *Ibid.*, p. 347.

Each has the quality of necessity yet together they locate the will, they make it finite, and, as aspects of the involuntary, they are part of the final necessity that informs any realistic doctrine of freedom. Character is defined as "the necessity closest to my will,"[26] that which limits man for the completion of every decision. Every act of the will is contingent upon the particularity of a character for its completion. Since one is not free to be someone else, to change his character according to desire, it is an aspect of necessity, an involuntary which cannot be altered. Although fascinated by Democritus' phrase, "man's character is his fate,"[27] Ricoeur does not simply wish a deterministic interpretation of character. For character is the location of human freedom.

I sense without being able to articulate it correctly that my character in its changeless aspects is only *my freedom's mode of being*.[28]

Ricoeur's reaction to the scientific study of character, the project undertaken by the esoteric Dutch school of ethology, is that although they are correct in seeing character as a major facet of the study of man, they are wrong in their use of an objective method which results in a deterministic view of man.[29] The consequence of that view, translated into philosophic language, is the failure to consider the inter-relation of voluntary processes in relation to character resulting in a hiatus between freedom and nature. Although the results of such studies are important, they must be restated in the language of the relation of the voluntary and the involuntary. Ultimately, philosophy must deal with the reconciliation of character with my character, and by this method understand realistically the relation of freedom and nature contained therein.

It may be difficult for an eidetic analysis to approach the notion of character, but certainly it is not as difficult as attempting to approach the unconscious. The difficulty that an interpretation of the unconscious presents, by definition, is that the unconscious is that of which we are not conscious. The purveyors of the doctrine of the unconscious teach that some of that which consciousness presents is false. The initial problem that a Freudian interpretation presents to phenomenology is that of rejecting the validity of consciousness. The phenomenological orientation rests its basic thesis, from Husserl on, on the validity of consciousness. As with the contribution of the other

[26] Ricoeur, *Freedom and Nature*, p. 355.
[27] *Ibid.*, p. 368.
[28] *Ibid.*
[29] Ricoeur relies on the findings of the Dutch school of ethology for a scientific analysis of character. (See *Ibid.*, pp. 357–64.)

sciences of man, so in this particular case, the fact that the scientific interpretation is not adequate from an eidetic perspective is not cause for its rejection but for its diagnostic interpretation. Ricoeur is critical of Freud, but he does not reject the theory of the unconscious; it undergoes reinterpretation. Ricoeur believes that the unconscious is the limit and boundary of freedom; the unconscious stands in relation to freedom (consciousness).[30] Ricoeur's criticism of the Freudian interpretation is three-fold. First, Freudian realism raises suspicions with regard to the reality of conscious experience. From a logical point of view this is spurious since the very idea of an interpretation of the unconscious enhances the status of consciousness. One must be conscious of the fundamental characteristic of the unconscious in order to grant it an interpretation. Hence, the Freudian thesis that the unconscious dominates consciousness is questionable. Second, associated with this realism is causalism, that is, the tendency to interpret facts of unconscious experience in terms of a causal scheme, concerned with objects and not in terms of the primal subjectivity of unconscious experience. The result is a *quasi-determinism*.[31] The issue here is a question of the language of causalism versus the language of intentionality. In the case of the latter, the primary reference is to consciousness, while in the case of the former, the language is one which refers to physical objects, a mental physics. The language of causalism is difficult because it dismisses freedom, and hence could be said to involve a total determinism. *"Causality is the objective equivalent of an absolutely unfree motivation."*[32] This concern is not a total loss for a proper understanding of freedom and nature, but from Ricoeur's perspective the language of causality requires translation into language which gives a just role to freedom, that is, the language of intentionality. Third, the problem with the unconscious is its genetic origin. It was Freud who originally discovered the unconscious, but he was informed by genetic principles of explanation, so the problem again was the attempt through an evolutionary model to explain higher forms of existence by lower forms and hence, from Ricoeur's perspective, to distort the true nature of consciousness.

With interpretations of the unconscious as with interpretations of character, Ricoeur's thesis remains the same, namely that an objective

[30] In his recent work, *De l'interprétation*, Ricoeur spends an entire volume developing a hermeneutic reinterpretation of Freud.
[31] Ricoeur, *Freedom and Nature*, p. 397.
[32] *Ibid.*

reading of character and an interpretation which gives primordial credence to the unconscious constitutes a death blow to freedom. "Any reading in the opposite direction, from character to will, from the unconsciousness to consciousness, represents a suicide of freedom which gives itself over to an object."[33] Yet criticism of the science of character and the unconscious does not constitute rejection. The aim of Ricoeur's analysis is constructive; his aim is to achieve by this diagnostic interpretation a more adequate understanding of nature. In this case the unconscious is to be understood as the "condition" of freedom.[34]

If character is understood as the necessity that is closest to the will, it is life which ranks along with character and the unconscious as the third realm of the involuntary, as the third force of necessity to be distinguished from the others as "basic necessity."[35] It is at the juncture of life that the ultimate paradox of freedom and necessity occurs because freedom is here "bound also to the pure fact of existing"[36] which is the final determination of freedom.

An analysis of life reveals three moments: structure, growth and birth. As structure, life is composed of biological functions which inform and limit freedom, yet functions which in a sense are not controlled by freedom. The nervous system, the endocrine system, etc., require little from the will to function properly. Life appears as a task resolved, which is something more than necessity. Life informs freedom. As structure, life is the *"condition sine qua non of will and of consciousness in general."*[37] Because of this paradoxical character of freedom and necessity, a final resolution of freedom and nature in terms of cosmology is impossible. There is a hiatus between freedom and nature and to resolve this falsely into a cosmology would be unrealistic. Instead they must be resolved by a human subject.

The second area where life poses the problem of the paradox of freedom and necessity is in growth, a process over which freedom has little if any control. "Growth is not my work. I experience it as a sheer fact."[38] Factors of growth, conceived as genetic growth, the development of personality, the limitations of age, are all part of the necessity to which freedom must acquiesce. Thirdly, if freedom is limited by life as struc-

---

[33] Ricoeur, *Freedom and Nature*, p. 407.
[34] *Ibid.*, p. 409.
[35] *Ibid.*,
[36] *Ibid.*, p. 414.
[37] *Ibid.*, p. 421.
[38] *Ibid.*, p. 425.

ture and growth, it is also limited by birth since each *Cogito* has no control over its origin. The striking problem presented by the physiological fact of birth is that birth is that phenomenon which consciousness cannot probe. An eidetic analysis which attempts to investigate the involuntary through the voluntary, upholding the primacy of consciousness, is baffled by the problem of birth which occurs in some sense prior to consciousness. Because of birth, heredity, the processes prior to the individual, and the limit placed upon the individual through birth, consent is introduced as a factor to which freedom must acquiesce.

Consent poses most radically the problem of the hiatus between freedom and nature. Through consent one is forced to acquiesce to that which most radically limits freedom presented as the limitation of character, the unconscious, and life. Philosophically understood, the problem that presents itself at this level is the mutual negation of freedom and nature and their projected resolution. The problem may be stated another way. Does Ricoeur's radical attempt to understand freedom (the voluntary) in relationship to nature (the involuntary) by considering freedom as an incarnate phenomenon run aground on the shoals of necessity? Does this solve the problem by a superficial doctrine of freedom? The hiatus may be stated through the bipolar doctrine of negation. Necessity negates freedom in its appearance as finitude of character, in the formlessness of the unconscious and in the contingency of life. Freedom responds to this radical limitation in a refusal which is affirmed by a wish for "totality"[39] which transcends the limitations of character, the unconscious and life, and in a wish for the "absolute freedom ... of total transparence."[40]

The question remains, how does one move from this double refusal which has its foundation in a double or bipolar negation to consent? Two options present themselves. Neither is adequate. Stoicism freely acquiesces to necessity by detachment, not by reconciliation. It simply accepts necessity by denying the role of the will. Orphism affirms necessity but in the process loses the self. It becomes fascinated with fate and it relegates the *self* to a secondary and inconsequent role. In contrast to stoicism with its negation and Orphism with its loss of self, Ricoeur understands the final resolution of freedom in hope, an eschatological dimension beyond the achievements of the eidetic method.

---

[39] Ricoeur, *Freedom and Nature*, p. 463.
[40] *Ibid.*, p. 464.

The final reciprocity of freedom and nature requires reflection beyond this present eidetic discussion.

4. *Freedom, Nature, and the Eidetic Method*

The content of Ricoeur's philosophical anthropology gives concrete direction for a correlation between mythic-symbolic language and philosophical anthropology. The primary questions center in the problem of the substantial content of philosophical anthropology in the context of the eidetic method. Under the predominant category "will" freedom has been the primary theme. This suggests the following conclusions. First, Ricoeur wishes to present a doctrine of freedom which is informed by nature. The desire to include nature within a doctrine of freedom arises, on the one hand, as an attempt to resolve the epistemological mind-body dualism and, on the other hand, to achieve something other than a nihilistic doctrine of freedom. Ricoeur's attempt to include scientific discussions of man, psychology, ethology, etc., may be understood to occur in the name of epistemology. From this perspective, the body is as much a constitutive aspect of knowledge as the mind because on the basis of the body mental decisions are formed and enacted. From an epistemological perspective, Ricoeur's revision of the mind-body problem is substantiated by the thesis that freedom is informed by nature and worked out by showing concretely how the involuntary is related to the voluntary. Ricoeur suggests that any realistic doctrine of freedom must be inclusive of an understanding of nature, but in a cosmological sense Ricoeur contains freedom within nature. In this quest for inclusion, one can perceive the source and direction of the global view. Yet, in this very quest freedom is limited.

If Ricoeur's first principle may be characterized as one which argues the case for nature as the informant of freedom, his second is that nature is the limit of freedom. The conclusion of *Freedom and Nature* is instructive in this regard. "An only human freedom"[41] is, for Ricoeur, a freedom which is limited by the context of its occurrence – the human and the involvement of the human in nature. The idea of a perfectly motivated freedom, or a freedom which is unlimited, is the opposite of an incarnate freedom which is governed and limited by the body. The original epistemological difficulty which may be understood to be resolved is replaced by the double negation of freedom and nature. Freedom is limited by nature and its problem. Freedom either rejects the

---

[41] Ricoeur, *Freedom and Nature*, p. 482.

very nature which informs it and shapes it, or it consents to necessity as the bond of freedom, but it is only on the basis of consent that freedom can be incarnate totally. For by consenting, one is acknowledging the nature that constitutes the very limit and bond of freedom.

However, human freedom can never be content with simple acquiescence to the necessity of nature. And this is the third principle of freedom: the final resolution of freedom with nature leads beyond nature. It is at this point that the concrete dynamic of Ricoeur's thought is stated. Part of Ricoeur's genius has been to see the limitations of the eidetic method. We can now state concretely the basis for that limitation. Husserl said that the eidetic method is concerned with man's fundamental possibilities – Ricoeur has extended that definition to include the body incarnate as the informant of those possibilities. But he has still operated within a fairly strict Husserlian orientation. Eidetics can provide us with the fundamental structures of willing. Yet eidetics deals with a pure description which excludes transcendence and fault. The paradox of freedom and nature in consent is the final achievement of the eidetic method and it is the point at which the method itself must be broken. It is at this juncture that a resolution beyond the immediate realm of willing is required. Freedom is limited. But freedom drives beyond limitation. This becomes a radical problem. Man's possible experience of rupture and his actual experience of evil lead to a drive toward transcendence which involves more than a neutral paradox of freedom and nature. The flow within man's being and man's seeming condemnation to evil posit the question of freedom. An anthropology which is concerned to understand fully freedom (its global character) moves beyond eidetics to language which contains man's own confession of his experience of evil and his desire to transcend it. The intermediate step is the specific existential experience which concretizes this movement.

B. FREEDOM AND FALLIBILITY

The transition from eidetic description to existential description is the movement from limitation by nature to limitation by fallibility. From the perspective of eidetics, the incarnate character of human freedom is both informant and limit, in the context of existential analysis, the problem of freedom is its limitation by fallibility. The achievement of the movement to existential description is significant from both the methodological point of view and from the total view of man. Methodologically, this movement constitutes the reintroduction of transcendence and fault which alters the doctrine of freedom by positing the radical reflective limit of fallibility. We have already seen that transcendence functions as a limit concept; fallibility does also. Both are included in the existential description.

The problem of the phenomenological method from Husserl on has been the establishment of the basis for reflection. Inasmuch as it is the body which functions as the informant of the will in Ricoeur's usage of the eidetic method, the body functions loosely as the pre-reflexive basis for reflection. Under existential description, it is an hypothesis about man which functions as the philosophical basis for reflection. The distinction is significant. For this type of description is transitional, a bridge between an eidetic and a hermeneutic method. Existential description thinks from the hypothesis which was stated by Plato through myth. A hermeneutic reflects from the symbol. Ricoeur points out that the reflective process is not thereby interrupted by this transition to existential description in the way that it is breached by the actuality of fault. If anything, this note of analysis paves the way for hermeneutic phenomenology.

The type of methodology chosen has direct bearing on the consequential view of freedom that will arise in the context of this global philosophic anthropology. The theme of freedom and nature is deepened by its plunge into the realm of ethics. The eidetic method can elaborate the fundamental possibilities of man; it can describe a freedom informed and limited by natrue, but existential analysis can go beyond this abstract description by elaborating the possibility of fallibility. The anthropological problem is much deeper at this level than one of methodology. Ricoeur wants to say the awareness of freedom is not given, rather it arises at the juncture of man's experience of himself. Without qualification, that is the most important distinction throughout this entire discussion of freedom. It is one thing to describe freedom as a constitutive aspect of willing under the rubric of decision, bodily motion and consent. It is quite another to specify the precise juncture where the consciousness of freedom arises. Freedom is not given for eidetic analysis; instead it must be discovered when one turns to man's actual self-experience. The specification of the juncture of freedom's entry into human consciousness can be construed as the pre-occupation of *Fallible Man*.

How does one discover freedom as a constitutive aspect of human

consciousness? Ricoeur's choice is to understand freedom in its reciprocal relationship to evil, which has as its consequence an ethical vision of the world.

We may understand by the ethical vision of the world our continual effort to
understand freedom and evil by each other.[42]

This elucidation provides the key to the manner in which the re-intro-
duced themes of transcendence and fault are to be handled. Their
relationship is reciprocal. It is only through a realistic understanding of
fallibility and fault that transcendence can be understood. Freedom is
seen in the context of its limitation because the awareness of freedom
arises through a penetration of fallibility and fault. If the orientation of
Fallible Man is to recover the meaning of fallibility and its location in
man's reflective experience of himself, this task is carried on in the
name of freedom. The concern of this section will be to capture the
precise and concrete meaning of freedom in relation to fallibility. This
can be done by referring briefly to the working hypothesis and by
following the movement toward concrescence through knowing, acting,
and feeling – the three-fold division of *Fallible Man*.

1. *The Hypothesis*

The idea that "man is by nature fragile and liable to err[43] plus the
idea that there is a "non-coincidence of man with himself"[44] suggests the
global view of man upon which *Fallible Man* is based. This dual hypothesis functioning as a pre-reflexive basis for reflection invites a delib-
eration which will specify fallibility as experience within a knowing-
acting-feeling consciousness. The fundamental motive guides the
reflection on this view of man as situated between finite and infinite
(Descartes), reason and desire (Plato), and the double infinite (Pascal).
If later the symbol invites thought, it would seem the assumption of
Fallible Man is that the hypothesis informs thought. It is by following
the basic themes presented in the hypothesis that one can engage in a
deepening reflection motivated toward the concrete, from consciousness to human consciousness, passing through knowing and acting, to
feeling where the actuality of fallibility is presented fully from the reflective standpoint. The hypothesis functions not as an ontology, but

---

[42] Paul Ricoeur, *Fallible Man*, trans. by Charles Kelbley (Chicago: Henry Regnery Co.,
1965), p. xxiv.
[43] *Ibid.*, p. 3.
[44] *Ibid.*, p. 4.

as a pre-reflexive invitation to thought which can bring forth conscious reflection without the possible obscuring of consciousness that an ontology could present. Ricoeur's distinctive rejection of a philosophical beginning and his reliance on an hypothesis as sufficient for the point of departure reflects emphatically the point of view stated in *Fallible Man*. Philosophy is "reflection on" something which it itself cannot provide.

2. *Epistemology and Fallibility*

If one takes reflection seriously, this attitude centers upon the constitutive character of consciousness. Reflection is first of all a matter of epistemology. Ricoeur maintains that originally reflection discovers primal finitude because thought begins with the object and it develops a point of view with regard to the object. Because it is limited first to that point of view, that is, to what is seen, this original act of consciousness is finite. Another way of stating the argument is to say thought begins with scission, inasmuch as it makes distinctions between objects by conceiving them from a perspective. In this sense thought is condemned originally to a finite point of view. This Humian discovery that thought begins with perception, according to Ricoeur, must be the beginning of an epistemology and not the end. The complement of this primordial sensibility is found in the Kantian distinction between sensibility and understanding. It is one thing to perceive, that may be the beginning of an epistemology; but it is another thing to understand or to reflect upon what is perceived. At this juncture Ricoeur introduces the signifying function of language. The use of language points to a transcendence of point of view by a linguistic incorporation of the entire object finitely perceived. For example, in the perception of a tree one receives a series of sense data – form, color, etc. One does not perceive the entire tree but only that which can be seen from a perspective, but the word tree transcends the particular perception to include reference to the entire thing. In this simple dialogue between seeing and saying, between sensibility and understanding, an epistemological version of the original hypothesis is demonstrated. This coalescence of finite and infinite, Ricoeur following Kant, calls the transcendental synthesis of pure imagination. This synthesis is only the final result of reflection. Initially what is revealed is the duality of finite and infinite.

Our reflection on the thing has given us an initial result: in discovering the breach between the finite and the infinite, it uncovered the "disproportion" between the verb which gives expression to being and truth at the risk of falling into error and, on the other hand, the passive look which is riveted to appearance and perspective.[45]

It is by a synthetic act of the imagination that that which is seen and which is understood (said) are held together. This unity is necessary in order that consciousness occur at all. Kant's criticism of an epistemology based solely upon sensation is that knowledge is more than Hume's notion of perception and ideas of perceptions. Whatever is known is known not simply through its objective appearance but also through what is contributed to that appearance by the imagination. Consciousness arises at the juncture of this synthesis between what is given by the object and what is given by the subject. Although Ricoeur is not entirely happy with the term a priori, he accepts this general epistemological position, regarding it as necessary for the development of a philosophical anthropology. It constitutes the epistemological basis for the original hypothesis. However, he is careful to suggest that this is primarily a matter for consciousness and not self-consciousness.

So we have first elaboration of that which could not be demonstrated through the limitations of eidetic analysis, namely the emergence of fallibility through reflection on an hypothesis which demonstrates initially, that is, epistemologically, a basic hiatus between that which is seen, perceived, and that which is understood, verbalized. On the epistemological level therefore, it is possible to demonstrate that man is that kind of being who is not only free to synthesize perspective and language through imagination, but also to acknowledge the disproportion between the two. In the latter sense there is a demonstrable disproportion within the self.

3. Action and Fallibility

Epistemology is concerned with the problem of the noetic base of consciousness. It is necessary in the construction of an anthropology of fallibility which has as its consequence the elaboration of the basic structures whereby a global anthropology of disproportion can be established. The leap from knowledge to action, the transition from theoretical to the practical, will follow the same basic scheme.

The finite aspect of the willing being is construed as character. The

---

[45] Ricoeur, *Fallible Man*, p. 57.

infinite is happiness with the synthesis of character and happiness in respect.

All the aspects of "practical" finitude that can be understood on the basis of the trancendental notion of perspective may be summed up in the notion of character. All the aspects of "practical" infinitude that can be understood on the basis of the transcendental notion of meaning may be summed up in the notion of happiness. The "practical" mediation which extends the mediation of the transcendental imagination, projected into the object, is the constitution of the person by means of "respect." This new analysis aims at showing the fragility of this practical mediation of respect, for which the person is the correlate.[46]

In *Freedom and Nature* Ricoeur defined character as the "necessity closest to my will"[47] because character was considered as that which limits man, a necessity to which freedom must consent. The designation of character as the practical correlate of finitude is not distant from that original description. Affective perspective (bodily feeling) plus practical perspective (habit-inertia and preservation) go together to make up character. Character suggests limit and limit suggests finitude. Man's character therefore is his limitation. Yet Ricoeur does not wish to present simply a negative doctrine of finitude inasmuch as finitude defined as character is not simply closure and necessity. Character is also the openness that makes freedom possible.

If one is to use the notion of a field of motivation, "Character is the zero origin of this field orientation; happiness is its infinite end."[48] Like the dialectic between saying and seeing, happiness transcends character as the aim of the individual beyond the limitation of the perspective of character.

To go back to a Kantian expression. . . I am the bearer of the "supreme destination of reason" in accordance with which I can "continue my existence." The idea of a complete volition and the destination of reason hallow an infinite depth in my desire, making it the desire for happiness and not merely the desire for pleasure.[49]

Character is man's original limitation but it is not his ultimate end. Happiness as a constitutive aspect of man's being, represents his quest for "totality," his desire to constitute himself beyond the limitation of character.

At this point disproportion introduces itself more radically than at the juncture of the distinction between sensibility and understanding

---

[46] Ricoeur, *Fallible Man*, p. 76–77 (Italics deleted).
[47] Ricoeur, *Freedom and Nature*, p. 355.
[48] Ricoeur, *Fallible Man*, p. 104.
[49] *Ibid.*, p. 103.

because here the disproportion is felt. Happiness exists as an unattained goal, an unfulfilled achievement. Even though this disjunction is present, even if the hypothesis that man is non-coincidence with himself is documented, Ricoeur wants to suggest that the total constitution of the person can never be discovered through the elucidation of the zero origin of character nor through the ultimate aim of happiness. They must be seen in unity, a unity that Ricoeur calls the practical synthesis of respect. Respect, Kant's term for the person, is the totality of the person as both origin and end, both finite and infinite, both character and happiness. In this manner the duality of the human person is synthesized and held to be a unity for in the act of respect the total person is sustained. As consciousness is synthesized in pure imagination so is the acting person synthesized in respect.

4. *Feeling*

The realm where the disproportion of man with himself is most completely internalized is the realm of feeling where Ricoeur contends the non-coincidence of man with himself is experienced most directly.

In advancing step by step from consciousness in general to self-consciousness and then to feeling, or in other words, from the theoretical to the practical to the affective, philosophical anthropology would progress toward a point which is at once more inward and more fragile.[50]

Feeling, the realm of the heart, is "the fragile moment *par excellence*."[51] The most clarifying understanding of feeling is given by Plato in the doctrine of *Thumos* wherein the image of the human subject as *Thumos* conceives man situated between reason and desire, eros and epithumia.[52] This disproportion and synthesis in the case of feeling, as in the case of knowing and doing, is bi-polar, and the dialectic is between the finitude of pleasure (desire) and the infinitude of happiness. Influenced by the definition of pleasure in Aristotle's *Nichomachean Ethics*, Ricoeur sees the finitude of pleasure in its blinding immediacy which has the reverse effect of cutting one off from life rather than fulfilling it. This does not mean that pleasure should be given a moralistic interpretation requiring it to be interpreted as evil; rather, it suggests that pleasure, when seen in relation to happiness, is that which limits man and grounds his finitude. The Greek theory of virtue associates pleasure

---

[50] Ricoeur, *Fallible Man*, p. 124.
[51] *Ibid.*
[52] *Ibid.*, p. 139.

with desire, but desire is not thereby negated because it must be related properly to reason or happiness. Pleasure receives its proper order in relation to happiness.

The specific fragility towards which feeling moves is internal conflict. "The disproportion between the principle of pleasure and the principle of happiness points up the truly human significance of conflict."[53] Conflict is best represented in three human passions: "having," "power," and "worth." In having (possession) "the relations of things govern most manifestly the relations of persons."[54] For the "I" is constituted by the mine. The conflict presented by having is that on the one hand man is limited by his possessions while on the other he is motivated towards an innocence of possession wherein he will, in an uncorrupt way, possess that which he needs without consequent economic domination. The passion for power presents a similar type of conflict, for particularly in political power violence of coercion is required and this is contrasted with a non-corrupt innocence, to be distinguished from corrupt (evil) power.[55] The third passion, the passion for esteem or worth, is limited by man's requiring it from others, while achieving self-esteem is subject to all possible corruptions.

In these three situations, the self finds itself in a continuous state of uncertainty, the consequence of which is indefiniteness. Here, the image changes slightly from that of the situation to that of mixture. Conflict points to mixture which is the basic composition of man's felt experience. The correlate to synthesis in knowing and doing is the center of conflict and mixture defined as feeling.

5. *Freedom and Fallibility*

Our program sought to understand freedom and fallibility in their reciprocal context in order to elucidate and elaborate the full meaning of freedom. Freedom is the essential theme of Ricoeur's work. *Fallible Man* is a specification of man's fallibility and not his freedom. That much is obvious inasmuch as the work is directed toward spelling out epistemologically, volitionally, and affectively how philosophical anthropology can describe man under the concept fallibility. It cannot be forgotten that the work itself is part of a larger corpus, the central theme of which is the will, and the original subject of which is freedom.

---

[53] Ricoeur, *Fallible Man*, p. 161.
[54] *Ibid.*, p. 172.
[55] *Ibid.*, p. 182.

The thesis of the first volume was that the limit and possibility of freedom was nature. Contextually interpreted, *Fallible Man* moves this analysis a step further. Rather than alter the theme, it deepens it by showing that man's limit and possibility is not simply nature. The limit of freedom is man's own propensity to fragility, his radical internal disproportion viewed distinctively on the noetic, acting, and feeling level. It is here that we are given an invitation to view the real limit of freedom, which must affect the will most radically.

To illustrate the role of freedom in this discourse on fallibility, one has to return to the global view and the quest for a total understanding of man. The two-fold characteristic of the three moments in the understanding of fallibility has been to see man as constituted between the extremes of transcendence and limitation, finite and infinite. Ricoeur makes this characteristic into a kind of Hegelian dialectic with originating affirmation, existential difference (and) human mediation.[56] All those forms which represent the transcendence of the finite toward an enduring freedom are classified as originating affirmation, inclusive of the infinite verb, the idea of happiness, and happiness of the heart. Existential difference is synonymous with those aspects of noetics, volition, and affective experience which together express limitation in the forms of character and pleasure.

Between these two characteristics (originating affirmation and existential difference) a full understanding of man and the possibility of fallibility begins to emerge as an option. In human mediation, which locates these extremes in man, one is enabled to understand both the totality of man's experience of himself as well as his possible limits. In a preliminary way, this seems to be the original program of the discussion, namely to see freedom and evil beside one another and in their mutual relation. But one cannot call factors of existential negation evil, for that would be to make finitude itself evil. However, it is possible to begin to understand the mutual penetration of this bi-polar theme. Fallibility can be seen best by viewing man as the mixture of affirmation and existential negation. Freedom is the backdrop against which fallibility is made clear and the theme of the work is sustained.

But one may question the authenticity of this approach. Can freedom really be understood apart from the encounter with its major adversary, evil? Is an anthropology truly global unless it has encountered a freedom which is spiritual and an evil which with radicality negates

[56] Ricoeur, *Fallible Man*, p. 207.

that freedom? That is the problem which is the basis for the drive toward a phenomenological hermeneutic.

C. FREEDOM AND FAULT

In the prior chapter Ricoeur's case for the phenomenological hermeneutic was analyzed. Commensurate with the purpose of the present discussion, we will examine the consequences of that hermeneutic for a global anthropology in symbol and myth. If the eidetic method can produce an understanding of freedom informed and limited by nature, and if the existential method can present an understanding of freedom tempered by fallibility, neither one is sufficiently concrete to deal with the real limit of freedom, that is, evil. It is this limit of phenomenological reflection that drives Ricoeur into the opaque, obscure but avowedly rich realm of religious discourse, namely the language of avowal, of the religious symbol and of myth. The logic of Ricoeur's major work *The Philosophy of the Will*, with its overall desire for the elaboration of a global view of man, has led to the phenomenological hermeneutic and the consideration of symbol and myth. Within the language of symbol and myth, it is in the language of avowal that this expression of evil is most concrete, but it is the language itself, not the abstract discourse that characterizes philosophic discussion, that is, the primal revelation of the symbol and interpretive discourse of myth which presents the concrete human expression of evil in a most direct fashion.

If in *Freedom and Nature* the pre-reflexive basis for reflection was the bodily involuntary (nature), and if in *Fallible Man* the pre-reflexive basis for reflection was the hypothesis, at the juncture of the phenomenological hermeneutic, the pre-reflexive basis for reflection is language itself. The term language requires careful definition, for by it Ricoeur means a very special type of language, the language of avowal, that is, the confession of the mythic-symbolic consciousness. To say that language functions as the pre-reflexive base for philosophical reflection means that whatever enters into the realm of philosophical thought does so because it is stimulated by the prior datum of language.

We have already seen the methodological consequences of this orientation but our present desire is to cast these consequences into the larger realm of the scope of Ricoeur's constructive work. Even though our final concern has been with Ricoeur's phenomenological hermeneutic wherein a positive correlation between mythic-symbolic language and philosophical anthropology is sustained, it has been necessary to consider the totality of his constructive thought to understand properly the context out of which the phenomenological hermeneutic is developed. The phenomenological hermeneutic dispenses neither with the problems of the *will*, nor with the problem of *freedom*, because the symbol and myth give concrete expression to freedom's encounter with evil.

It is important that the stake of the phenomenological hermeneutic be understood properly. The discussions in *Freedom and Nature* and *Fallible Man* are avowedly abstract for they deal with possibilities only. Even fallibility is finally postulated only as a possibility. The advantage of this *tour de force* into the realm of language is that it avails the philosopher of a direct experience, that which reflection cannot attain on its own.

For Ricoeur there are three types of language in the realm of discourse on evil: (1) a primary language related to symbols, the most elemental and central of expressions about evil; (2) a language of symbolic interpretation in myth which depends on the primary symbols of which it is an elaboration; (3) a language of philosophical interpretation which is fundamentally speculative in its consideration of the problem of evil. The argument for going to the primacy of the symbol as the original and most elemental expression of the consciousness of evil is that ordinary philosophical discourse is too abstract to entertain the primary utterance given by the religious confession of evil in symbol. "We must proceed regressively and revert from the 'speculative' expressions to the 'spontaneous' ones."[57] The temptation of the philosopher who wishes to deal with the problem of evil is to go immediately to the theological doctrine of original sin, the doctrine which has claimed to be the rational explanation of evil in western thought. Yet the doctrine of original sin is rational only in appearance. That explanation of the origin of evil is itself dependent both on the gnostic period in which it was formed and the prior experience which it attempts to explain. Ricoeur argues that it is necessary to get behind this pseudo-rational expression in order to discover directly the encounter of consciousness with evil. It is to the symbol and the associated language of the symbol that Ricoeur's thought under the rubric of the phenomenological hermeneutic is directed originally. It is this most primary of

---

[57] Paul Ricoeur, *The Symbolism of Evil*, trans. by Emerson Buchanan (New York, Evanston, and London: Harper and Row, Publishers, 1967), p. 4.

languages that necessitates an original consideration. At this point freedom undergoes its most radical test.

1. *Symbol and the Servile Will*

The first consequence of Ricoeur's investigation of symbol for a global anthropology is the consideration of the symbols of evil in the context of a servile will.[58] Because the concept is based on a phenomenological analysis of the symbols of evil and not on speculation itself, as with the concept of fallibility, the notion of servile will is only indirectly available. This fact alone justifies the investigation of symbolism which takes one from the possibility of fallibility to the actual experience of fault confessed in language. To understand this consequence of the phenomenological investigation of symbols it is necessary to turn to the symbols themselves.

As already indicated, the symbols of stain, of sin, and of guilt are the most appropriate for the confession of evil (in western history). None of these symbols is simply available to philosophic reflection in the sense that they have to be discussed imaginatively and re-enacted in consciousness in order to be understood. The hermeneutic task at this important elemental level is to attempt to point to the basic characteristics of the symbols through a stance of empathy. Given this context, the claim is made that an intentional analysis can discern the basic characteristics of these three primary symbols.

a. Stain. The intentional analysis of stain reveals that stain has two distinct traits. Objectively perceived it is a "something that infects,"[59] subjectively understood it is a "dread that anticipates the unleashing of . . . avenging wrath."[60] Ricoeur understands the unique characteristic of the symbol, when seen in relationship to rational modes of thought, to be its multivalence, or its double intentionality. This two-fold characteristic is seen in defilement as the literal meaning of spot or stain, that from which one desires cleansing, and as the symbolic sense, constituted through the literal sense, of the impure or the symbolic defilement. This double characteristic of stain is perhaps best borne out in rituals of absolution which are instituted in order to rid the practitioner of the literal spot and to cleanse him from the fear and terror that the spot symbolizes. Ricoeur finds a great similarity between Hebrew

---

[58] Ricoeur, *The Symbolism of Evil*, p. 151.
[59] *Ibid.*, p. 33.
[60] *Ibid.*

rituals of cleansing and the Greek practice of catharsis. Both are aimed at ridding man of the evil brought on by the presence of stain.

b. Sin. The symbol of "stain" in relation to "sin" is held to be more archaic, though not necessarily in an historical sense, while sin retains most of the basic themes that are present in stain. The transition from defilement or stain to sin is both continuous and discontinuous. The continuity can be affirmed in terms of factors of fear, impurity, etc. The fundamental distinction, however, comes in terms of the internalization that is characteristic of sin as opposed to the externalization that is an aspect of defilement. Ricoeur finds sin to be most distinctly the rupture of a relationship best defined in terms of the Hebrew covenant theology revealed in the Old Testament. The rupture of a relationship between the divine, which may or may not be monotheistic, and the human has as its consequence the inauguration of divine wrath, which, Ricoeur holds, is the subjective side of the symbol of sin while the infinite demand-finite commandment is the objective correlative. Like stain, sin has a literal characteristic as well as a symbolic one. The symbolism of sin carries on the major intention of the symbolism of stain. From the viewpoint of cycle and return that is part of the Old Testament prophecy, sin is seen as a kind of retreat into nothingness. But sin is something. Sin is positive because it is posited, and in this sense this symbol is comparable directly to the symbolism of stain. This is the realism of sin directly associated with its literal character. Sin is like stain in that it can be understood in relation to its opposite. As the opposite of defilement is purity, so the opposite of sin is redemption.

c. Guilt. If stain, sin, and guilt were placed on a continuum, the points of which were the external and the internal, Ricoeur finds guilt to be the most radically internal. It is in this sense that the continuity between guilt and the prior symbols can be affirmed. Defilement expresses man's encounter with evil as a stain or spot, thereby affirming the precedence of evil. Sin tends to express this same encounter in terms of the "unhappy consciousness" elicited in the category of "before God" and the breach of the covenant relationship. Guilt expresses this same encounter with and confession of evil in terms of a radical individuation directly associated with the Greek development of penal law and the development of the scrupulous conscience among the Pharisees. Having defined guilt in relationship to the Greek penal interpretation and the Pharisaical interpretation, the opportunity is presented to turn to the classical Pauline interpretation of the law which borrows from both traditions and which Ricoeur considers significant for the depth of its vision.[61] "The promotion of guilt marks the entry of man into the circle of condemnation; the meaning of that condemnation appears only after the event to the 'justified' conscience."[62] It is only on the basis of the Pauline interpretation of justification that the full meaning of the law and guilt before the law is fully understood.

2. The Symbols and the Servile Will

How does one arrive at a notion of a captive freedom which is the larger issue of the investigation of freedom? Although the three symbols do not present rationally the idea of a slave-will, Ricoeur affirms that that is their basic intentionality and their anthropological significance. Since the symbols have a similar structure, even though there are significant distinctions, it is possible to show that they all may be correlated in relation to this captive freedom.

Ricoeur argues in his conclusion of the discussion of the servile will that in the three characteristics of the symbol stain it is possible to recapitulate the basic structure of the symbolism of evil as it pertains to the servile will.[63] First, defilement demonstrates that evil is not a nothing. It is positive because it is a something done, achieved, and conquered whether viewed on a human or a divine scale. Second, evil is seen as something that comes to man from the outside; as that which was present before man and is thereby a structure in which man participates. Third, evil is something which infects, which is thereby a contagious phenomenon. Aspects of this three-fold scheme are presented in the other symbols and together they point to something more than fallibility. They suggest an evil which surrounds human freedom, which comes before man, which infects him and thereby limits his ability for doing that good he may choose, and yet with all its precedence, he commits evil. The discussion of freedom with which Ricoeur's work began is carried a step further into the realm of the radical limitation presented by evil. This cannot be regarded as a full interpretation of the problem to which evil points. Myths, the primitive hermeneutic of symbols, carry the discussion a step further. For that reason it is necessary to turn to the myths of evil.

---

[61] See Romans, particularly chapter 7.
[62] Ricoeur, The Symbolism of Evil, p. 150.
[63] See the discussion on servile will in The Symbolism of Evil. pp. 151–57.

D. MYTH AND THE PROBLEM OF EVIL

Ricoeur's definition of myth as the primitive hermeneutic of symbol implies that the change in discussion from symbol to myth simply involves a further and more comprehensive elaboration of the basic issues involved in symbol. The discussion of myth will have as its consequence a more complete analysis of the basic problem of freedom and evil.

For Ricoeur myth can be defined in a three-fold way: first, as that which unites man in an exemplar history, thereby giving a definition to man and humanity; second, myth tells a story which combines fable and history; and third, myth attempts to explain the enigma of human history, placing within its story the explanation for man's particular problem.

Ricoeur places himself solidly in the tradition of those thinkers who, like Eliade, find myth to be a form of meaningful discourse. He is radically opposed to that group who make myth a "falsity." For Ricoeur, myth, like symbol, informs thought. Through the development of a hermeneutic proper to myth this position can be sustained. The issue of a proper interpretation can be shown best by juxtaposing myth and gnosis, a juxtaposition which has been the axiological basis for the disposal of myth in western philosophical history. "The principal objection that philosophy addresses to myth is that the mythical explanation is incompatible with the rationality discovered or invented by the Pre-Socratics, from that time on, it represents the simulacrum of rationality."[64] Ricoeur's answer to this kind of criticism is significant. "My working hypothesis is that criticism of the pseudo-rational is fatal not to myth but to gnosis."[65] What Ricoeur wishes to do at this point is to disassociate myth and gnosis to show how myth can operate as the informant of knowledge.

Ricoeur's study of myth is not a study of myth in general but an analysis of myths which portray the origin and end of evil. To that end he designates certain characteristics (considered earlier in another context) of the myths of evil, characteristics which, when developed fully, constitute a basic typology of that particular kind of myth. For Ricoeur myths of the origin and the end of evil constitute four types: myths of creation, fall, tragedy, and exile. The myths of creation con-

[64] Ricoeur, *The Symbolism of Evil*, p. 164.
[65] *Ibid.*

strue the origin of evil as "coextensive with the origin of things."[66]
The gods of the myth struggle with chaos which is synonymous with the
power of evil, and creation is the consequence. In this mythic scheme,
salvation is identical with creation. The myths of the fall of man designate that fall as an "irrational event,"[67] in the context of a completed
creation. Ricoeur believes that salvation in this context becomes historical. Between the myths of creation and fall Ricoeur places the
myths that can be called tragic. Here guilt and fault are not synonymous with an irrational act but with the very fact of existing. Here freedom coincides with necessity. Finally, there is that Ricoeur wants to
call "the myth of the exiled soul."[68] This is the myth which separates
soul and body, the myth upon which much of Greek speculation has
been dependent.

Although no purpose would be served in discussing all those myths
in explicit detail, they can be specified more concretely by reference to
their sources. From Ricoeur's perspective, the creation myth can be
characterized as a myth arising among the Sumer-Akkadians which
saw chaos as anterior to order, seeing evil as co-extensive with the generation of the divine. This myth, sustained by a ritual repetition
emphasized in the Babylonian New Year's festival, was retained in a
recessive form in the Hebrew kingship festival. Aspects of it can even
be found in the sagas of Homer and Hesiod. The tragic myth Ricoeur
sees as primarily Greek, although aspects of it – pre-tragic themes –
can be discovered in many cultures where fault "is traced back into the
divine and . . . this divine initiative works through the weakness of man
and appears as divine possession."[69] Ricoeur, however, finds in Aeschy-
lus the coalescence of the tragic themes of blindness sent by the gods of
jealousy and immoderation. He added to the theme of predestination of
evil "The anthropological theme of 'heroic' greatness."[70] The primary
source for the myth of the fall is the Adam myth, which, as we have seen,
combines the distinctive themes of the other myths while adding its
own particular historical and eschatological vision. The final myth, the
myth of the exiled soul, finds its source in archaic Orphism which develops an anthropological dualism. Because of its use by Plato, it is
perhaps one of the most important from the perspective of western
intellectual history.

[66] Ricoeur, *The Symbolism of Evil*, p. 172.
[67] *Ibid.*
[68] *Ibid.*, p. 174.
[69] *Ibid.*, p. 213.
[70] *Ibid.*, p. 218.

1. *The Cycle of Myths*

The most important conclusion Ricoeur comes to with regard to the study of myth is the dynamic interpretation of myths. The four myths he has studied are brought together in the Adam myth. The hermeneutic basis for this attempt, as we have seen, is called a wager and has no complete objective justification. Ricoeur, standing in the western Christian tradition, is influenced by his own allegiance to the Christian faith. But the case for this dynamic interpretation of myth does have other foundations. The movement from the static interpretation (interpretation of myths in terms of themselves) to the dynamic interpretation (interpretation in terms of the Adam myth) is sustained by the argument that the Adam myth is still very much alive in the western tradition. By turning to the Adam myth as the central myth, it is possible to sustain better the case for the significance of myth as a source for thought. Another argument relates to the significance of the Adam myth itself. The Adam myth has its own intrinsic validity and because of its universal character takes into itself significant aspects of all other myths. It is possible to argue that stress on the significance of the Adam myth does not mean the abolishment of all other myths.

The significance of the tragic myth is found in its portrayal of the priority of evil as something which is not posited by man's use and misuse of freedom. It is the symbol of the serpent in the Adam myth which retains this version of the priority of evil. In the Biblical tradition, the Job story is based on elements of the tragic theme. There are elements of hostility between the Adam myth and the tragic myth, and whereas the tragic myth finds its justification in a capricious deity, the Adam myth affirms the goodness of God. And whereas the final end of the tragic myth is said to be condemnation, the final end of the Adam myth is salvation. Even though these elements of conflict are presented in man's confession of evil, in the Biblical myth there is testimony to the evil he did not create. It is on that ground that the Adam myth can be said to take into itself elements of the tragic myth.

The myth of chaos, or what Ricoeur calls the theogonic myth, sustains the same fundamental characteristics as does the myth of tragedy but places evil as a phenomenon prior to man's experience of it. This divine assumption of tragedy is taken up into the Adam myth. Ricoeur believes that the Adam myth is completed in the myth of the Second Adam who does include this factor of tragedy in the form of the suffering servant.

Ricoeur's dynamic consideration of myth concludes with the interpretation of the exiled soul in relation to the Adam myth. As with the other myths, in the myth of the exiled soul, the experience of evil is already there.

Our starting point must once again be the experience of evil, as already there – that is to say, the other side of the Adamic myth, the side represented by Eve and the Serpent. But, while the tragic myth interprets passivity and reduction in terms of *divine* blinding and the theogonic myth interprets them in terms of resurgence of *primordial* chaos, the Orphic myth develops the aspect of the apparent externality of the reduction and tries to make it coincide with the "body," understood as the unique root of all that is involuntary.[71]

It is this phenomenon of the root of evil in the externality of the body that is present in the secondary symbols of Hebraic-Christian literature. The symbols of captivity, of Exodus, Babylonian Exile, the prophetic vision of divine condemnation, Pauline discussions of the sin captive within the body, all represent aspects of Orphic symbolism. But like the analysis of the Adamic myth in relation to other myths, Ricoeur finds that the Adam myth reinterpreted in a Christian context leads one out of the dualism of the body and soul to their reconciliation.

Ricoeur has suggested that freedom and evil must be understood by one another. Both the symbols and the myths are concerned as directly with freedom as they are with evil. The discussion of symbol and myth presents a problem for the overall interpretation of the theme of freedom, the subject that dominates the entire philosophical anthropology. Ricoeur has refused to understand the investigation into language as simply a problem of a hermeneutic but rather the anchor of a hermeneutic is philosophical anthropology. Innovations in the interpretation of language are a contribution to the understanding of man. The interpretation of the symbols and myths of evil coalesce with the fundamental themes of Ricoeur's entire work. The original concern of *The Philosophy of the Will* was to understand the function of willing under the tripart formula – I decide, I move my body, I consent. In each case, this three-fold movement shows the voluntary as informed and limited by the involuntary. The doctrine of freedom that occurs as a consequence is one fully informed and limited by nature but not yet restricted by a radical encounter with evil. With the consideration of man under the rubric of fallibility, the possibility of falling under the radical limit of evil is entertained only as a possibility introduced by a hypothetical consideration. The leap into the realm of mythic-symbolic discourse must be justified on the basis of a philosophic investigation

[71] Ricoeur, *The Symbolism of Evil*, p. 331.

that desires a total understanding of man, and because of the basic movement of Ricoeur's thought toward the concrete.

It seems that this consideration affords one important conclusion. The logic of Ricoeur's work suggests that a *global anthropology has as a concrete correlate dimension a mythic-symbolic language*. But this conclusion may be inverted. *A mythic-symbolic language is necessary for a full philosophical anthropology.* That is the subject of this essay and it seems amply documented by this investigation into the constructive work of Paul Ricoeur. In contrast to the view of mythic-symbolic language established earlier, this approach assumes that mythic-symbolic language is *necessary*. But Ricoeur's thought is difficult precisely at this point of the explanation of the necessity. To see the significance of the turning toward mythic-symbolic language, it was imperative that we cover the scope of his philosophical anthropology. We can now see that mythic-symbolic language is employed in the name of freedom and its limit, the central theme of his work.

IV

HERMENEUTIC PHENOMENOLOGY
AND LANGUAGE

The recent developments of Paul Ricoeur's thought are consistent with the basic methodological and anthropological themes outlined in the prior discussion. And yet there is one significant development beyond *The Symbolism of Evil*, namely the incorporation of a hermeneutic method into an entire philosophic program which extends beyond the analysis of religious symbol and myth. This can be shown through consideration of a number of related philosophical problems and solutions: the hermeneutic definition of philosophy, the subject matter of philosophy as language, an engagement with other human sciences that have the interpretation of language as their subject matter, a definition of philosophy as a reflective task, and finally the centralization of all these issues in the persistent question that continues to dominate Ricoeur's thought – who is man? Ricoeur's view of the philosophical task culminates in the phrase, the archaeology of the subject.[1]

There are three areas in which we wish to examine the later development of Ricoeur's thought: first, language and hermeneutic theory in the context of the debate with Freud; second, considerations of the phenomenology of language in the context of the debate with structuralism; and third, an examination of Ricoeur's contribution to hermeneutics conceived in relationship to central figures in the history of that discussion.

This analysis concludes the consideration of Ricoeur, while at the same time, it lays the foundation for the final constructive statement of the problem of mythic-symbolic language and philosophical anthropology. As a conclusion to the analysis of Ricoeur, it illustrates the possibility that the hermeneutic of language has as a potential philosophical position. It lays the foundation for the constructive dis-

---

[1] The phrase "archaeology of the subject" is introduced by Ricoeur as the consequence of his dialogue with Freud. Further discussion of this phrase will occur later in the chapter.

cussion by establishing a broad context, inclusive of a general consideration of language and anthropology, for a positive correlation between mythic-symbolic language and philosophical anthropology.

A. PHILOSOPHY AS A HERMENEUTIC

The proposition that emerges from *The Philosophy of the Will* is that the study of the particular language of the symbol is necessary for a full, global understanding of man. In this case a hermeneutic is invoked for a very special reason; it is necessary because through that method of interpretation the philosopher can understand symbolism and mythology. The later writings of Ricoeur suggest that the hermeneutic task has become generalized into a philosophical program which defines, in part, the nature of philosophy itself. It can be stated in retrospect that in the movement from eidetics to a hermeneutic Ricoeur has found that a hermeneutic as a motif for philosophical elaboration is the most satisfactory for the basic themes of a philosophical anthropology. If the central task of philosophy is to seek a global understanding of man on the basis of particular hermeneutic investigations, then the task of the hermeneutic can be broadened to consider not only the hermeneutic of myth and symbol, but also the interpretation of other related symbolic forms. Therefore, if he chooses to expand his philosophical program by moving in the direction of a philosophical consideration of psychoanalysis, one may consider this an extension of the initial hermeneutic program. If it can be maintained that psychoanalysis works with linguistic data in the form of symbols as its subject matter, and that psychoanalysis involves itself in a task of interpretation, then the meaning of a hermeneutic may be broadened to include a consideration of psychoanalysis.

There are important consequences of this view. For Ricoeur this results in a reappraisal of the function of consciousness in the context of philosophy. A hermeneutic as the methodological foundation for a philosophical program suggests that the task of philosophy is one of mediation inasmuch as consciousness is not immediately given. The significance of this point will be examined later in a discussion of the reflective task of philosophy. It is sufficient here to suggest that philosophy, hermeneutically conceived, has a specific purpose, an ethical purpose. Following Spinoza, Ricoeur conceives the aim of such a philosophical program to be the consideration of the ultimate destiny of man.

Ethics completes philosophy. So conceived, philosophy cannot be a matter of intuition.

> We are now ready to complete our negative proposition – reflection is not intuition – by a positive proposition; reflection is the appropriation of our effort to exist and our desire to be, through the works which witness to this effort and this desire; this is why reflection is more than a simple critique of knowledge, and even more than a simple critique of moral judgment; prior to any critique of judgment, it reflects on this act of existing which we unfold in effort and in desire.[2]

The hermeneutic becomes an existential act because interpretation is a matter of the very definition of man.

If a hermeneutic is the methodological foundation for the task of philosophy in Ricoeur's later writings, the study of language may be said to be its object. The difference between the study of language in *The Symbolism of Evil* and in those later wirtings is not one of changing attitudes; rather the study of language becomes the point of convergence, the subject matter of philosophy per se.

> It seems to me that it is a domain in which all philosophical inquiries nowadays are blending, that of language. It is there that the investigations of Wittgenstein, the linguistic philosophy of the English, the phenomenology issuing from Husserl, the research of Heidegger, the works of the Bultmannian and other schools of New Testament exegesis, the works of comparative history of religions and anthropology bearing on myth, rite and belief, – and finally psychoanalysis, all cross one another.[3]

The study of language converges in the studies of the human sciences: at least those which have the study of language as their subject matter.

In this discussion we wish to raise the question of the extent to which Ricoeur's theory of language has changed or developed in the writing of *De l'interprétation*. Although Ricoeur's theory of language has deepened, the basic foundations are implicit in *The Symbolism of Evil* because the theory of language is informed by the theory of symbol. The problem of language, so construed, is that of its double character, technically the distinction between univocal and equivocal discourse. There are two modes of discourse, that with singular intentionality, and language, which has a double intention. The basis for this view is already established in *The Symbolism of Evil* in Ricoeur's "criteriology" of symbols. In the later work, however, this view is set more clearly in the context of alternatives.

In *De l'interprétation* Ricoeur juxtaposes his theory of symbol to

---

[2] Paul Ricoeur, "Herméneutique et réflexion," *Demitizzazone E Immagine* (Padova Ce dam-Casa Editrice Dott. Antonie Milani, 1962), p. 31.

[3] Paul Ricoeur, *De l'interprétation, essai sur Freud* (Paris: Editions du Seuil, 1965). p. 12.

two other views, one of which is too "narrow" while the other is too "large." Ricoeur criticizes Cassirer's definition of symbol because it occurs as a basis for an entire epistemology. Cassirer speaks of the "symbolic function" by which he means the mode whereby consciousness constructs a universe of perception and discourse. For Cassirer the primary characteristic of the symbol is its ability to synthesize. In Ricoeur's terms, Cassirer simply collapses the distinction between the univocal and the equivocal.

In unifying all the functions of mediation under the title of symbol, Cassirer gives an amplitude to the concept equal to the concepts of reality on the one hand and of culture on the other. Thus a fundamental distinction is dissipated, which constitutes in my eyes a veritable divide: between univocal expressions and multivalent expressions.[4]

This epistemological view of the symbol is too simple and too general.

As in *The Symbolism of Evil*, but with more serious consideration given to epistemology, Ricoeur defines the symbol on the basis of insights given through studies in history and phenomenology of religion. Ricoeur believes that it is Eliade's *Patterns in Comparative Religion* that does justice to the particularity of the symbol, inasmuch as each example of cosmic symbolism has a double signification. That double signification is the careful association of literal and symbolic elements.

...whether it pertains to the symbolism of the sky as figure of the very high and immense, of the powerful and unchangeable, of the sovereign and the sage, or the symbolism of vegetation which is born, dies, and is reborn, of water which threatens, cleans or vivifies, these innumerable theophanies or hierophanies are an inexhaustible source of symbolization.[5]

The problem with Cassirer's view is that in it everything becomes a symbol, in the sense that all distinctions between types of discourse are lost. Because of his neo-Kantian view of the symbol as the epistemological foundation for the unity of thought, the distinctiveness of particular symbols, that is, cosmic symbols, psychic symbols, etc., is lost. As such this definition of symbol is too broad.

In contrast to this overly broad view of the symbol Ricoeur presents his critique of analogy and the analogical view of the symbol as too narrow. Such a view is too narrow because it separates the literal intention from the symbolic intention of the symbol. This limitation, of course, has already been developed in our previous discussions. However, in *De l'interprétation* our author has wished to develop the central motif "the symbol invites thought" by suggesting that the

---

[4] Ricoeur, *De l'interprétation*, p. 21.
[5] *Ibid.*, p. 23.

transition from the literal to the symbolic intentionality initially involves one in problems of language and interpretation. It is in this context that the solution to the overly broad and the overly narrow view of the symbol occurs. This solution takes into account the act of interpretation.

I would say that there is a symbol there when the linguistic expression lends itself through its double meaning or its multiple meanings to a task of interpretation. What sets up this task is an *intentional structure which does not consist in the correspondence of the meaning to the thing, but in an architecture of meaning, in a correspondence of meaning to meaning, of the second meaning to the first meaning, whether this correspondence be or not analogy, whether the first meaning conceals or reveals the second meaning.* It is this texture which makes possible the interpretation, although only the effective movement of interpretation makes it manifest.[6]

In this sense the investigation of the symbol is radically tied to the renewal of language and the necessity of a hermeneutic inasmuch as a hermeneutic involves the very transition from the literal to the symbolic. Equally, a hermeneutic becomes a part of man's being, for it is by entering into the process of interpretation that language, and therefore being, is restored. The anthropological side of this principle will be discussed later.

At any rate we are now in a position to understand why language is even more directly the subject matter of philosophy. Given the original distinction between language as univocal and language as multivalent, a distinction grounded in the theory of the symbol, Ricoeur has found that it is possible and necessary for reflection on the symbol to be a means to the entry into language.

We are at present in search of a broad philosophy of language which would account for the multiple functions of human signification and their mutual relations.[7]

However, neither hermeneutic nor linguistic considerations as they constitute Ricoeur's proposal for philosophy explain why the phenomenologist should engage a psychoanalyst in dialogue, yet the theme of *De l'interprétation* is a consideration of the works of Freud. To the practicing phenomenologist a consideration of the relationship between psychology and phenomenology should come as no surprise. It was the psychologist, Franz Brentano, Husserl's professor, who developed the doctrine of intentionality, one of the cardinal doctrines of phenomenology. It is also true that Husserl thought more highly of

---

[6] Ricoeur, *De l'interprétation*, pp. 26–27.
[7] *Ibid.*, p. 13.

Brentano than he did of any of his other professors. Beyond that, it is true that psychology and phenomenology have maintained a continuously close, though occasionally strained, relationship. With regard to American phenomenology and psychology, Herbert Spiegelberg claimed:

As far as psychology is concerned, one might well maintain that phenomenology has arrived in the American world, much more than it has in American philosophy, where it is still largely considered an exotic plant. Thus, in a recent symposium on behaviorism and phenomenology at Rice University, sponsored by the American Psychological Association, phenomenology was given equal ranking with behaviorism, apparently one of the two major alternatives in psychology today.[8]

Inasmuch as this statement illustrates the continuing close relationship between phenomenology and psychology, it should come as no surprise to the phenomenologist at least that Ricoeur has chosen to take up the debate with psychology and one of the most important figures in psychology and psychoanalysis. The history of the phenomenological movement suggests the possibility of such an attempt.

The reasons for the consideration of Freud by Ricoeur are found in the development of *The Philosophy of the Will* itself and its program for a philosophical anthropology. If it is true that the overall task of that work is to establish a truly global understanding of man, and if the consequence of that proposition is the necessary investigation of special languages, then it follows that other languages beside the language of religious symbols and religious myths require investigation. Second, if symbolism constitutes the basis for the possible repossession of language, then the investigation of other symbolisms is both legitimate and necessary. *The Symbolism of Evil* was predicated on the basis of the investigation of data from one human science, the history of religions. But a number of disciplines converge on the investigation of language: psychoanalysis, the history of religions, anthropology, linguistics, sociology, etc. Equally, each of these disciplines converges in its attempt to understand the nature of man. Each discipline is concerned with a special language, or the relationship between language and human understanding. Of course, this is not the disciplines' entire motivation, but it is conceivable that this is part of their task. If philosophy incorporates a hermeneutic foundation, then an investigation of other special languages is not beyond its purview. Third, Ricoeur's definition of the symbol has three dimensions: the cosmic, the oneiric, and the

---

[8] Edward N. Lee and Maurice Mandelbaum, eds., *Phenomenology and Existentialism* (Baltimore: The Johns Hopkins Press, 1967), p. 219.

poetic. Generally, the symbolism of evil represents an investigation into cosmic symbolism. Yet, an intrinsic dimension of every symbolism is its oneiric dimension. Therefore, an investigation of that discipline, which has as its central focus and investigation of the symbolic content of dreams, is germane to the general philosophic study of symbolism. Fourth, the present discussion of psychoanalysis in France has made this discussion possible. Jacques Lacan has, according to principles derived from structuralism, defined psychoanalysis as a type of language. In his work *Écrits*, psychoanalysis becomes the analysis of a symbolism. He states:

It is, we know, in the experience inaugurated by psychoanalysis that one can comprehend through what subterfuges of the imaginary this grip of the symbolic comes to be exercised, even to the most intimate depths of the human organism.[9]

This major analysis of Freud has placed psychoanalysis in a new light. The context for interpretation becomes one of symbolism and language. Succinctly, the task of *De l'interprétation* is to open again the problem of the *The Symbolism of Evil: "to know the relation between a hermeneutics of symbols and a concrete philosophy of reflection."*[10] The analysis of Freud will further the understanding of that relationship.

In meeting this task Ricoeur does not wish to usurp the role of the psychologist or the psychoanalyst. As we shall see in the discussion of the task of reflective philosophy, it is for philosophical reasons, for reasons emerging from *The Philosophy of the Will*, that such an enterprise is attempted.

This book is not a book of psychology but of philosophy. It is the new comprehension of man introduced by Freud which concerns me.[11]

One of the prerequisites for this dialogue is the assumption that psychoanalysis and phenomenology are involved in analogous tasks. If language is the subject matter of both, that claim may in part be maintained. But if the claim is to be sustained there must be a methodological analogy. The task then is to show that psychoanalysis is analogous to a hermeneutic, a task which becomes one of the major objectives in the interpretation of Freud. In part the problem is one of defining the Freudian enterprise. Is it based on the so-called objective norms of empirical science, or is it a subjective science which requires a correlate subjective interpretation? Ricoeur wants to make the case

[9] Jacques Lacan, *Écrits* (Paris: Aux Editions du Seuil, 1966), p. 11.
[10] Ricoeur, *De l'interprétation*, p. 8.
[11] *Ibid.*

that psychoanalysis is based upon subjective interpretations, and to that extent it employs something like a hermeneutic.

As soon as that association is made the problem of distinguishing the type of hermeneutic employed becomes important. In *The Philosophy of the Will* Ricoeur involved himself in a specification of the meaning of a hermeneutic. In his more recent writings. Ricoeur has clarified hermeneutic alternatives. Concretely the hermeneutic of language presents a double possibility which occurs as the consequence of our modernity.

It is necessary that we be placed from the beginning in the face of this double possibility: this tension, this extreme traction is the most truthful expression of our "modernity"; the predicament which is made of language at present, carries this double possibility, this double solicitation, this double urgency: on the one hand, to purify discourse of its excrescences, liquidate the idols, go from inebriety to sobriety forming once and for all the balance of our poverty; on the other hand, to have recourse to the most "nihilistic" movement, the most destructive, the most iconoclastic, in order to *let speak* what once, what each time has been *said* when the meaning appeared anew, when the meaning was full; it seems to me hermeneutics is driven by this double motivation; willingness to suspect, willingness to listen; vow of rigor, vow of obedience; we are today the men who have not finished killing the *idols* and who scarcely begin to understand the symbols. Perhaps this predicament, in its apparent distress is instructive: perhaps the extreme iconoclasm pertains to the restoration of meaning.[12]

This double possibility occurs because of the multiplicity of modern disciplines which have reflection as their foundation, that is, reflection on a particular set of phenomena.

But within that possibility occurs a dichotomy of hermeneutic types. It would be unfair to say that of the two modern hermeneutic schools one is totally reductionistic and the other is the opposite. Since a hermeneutic is a reflection on a particular set of data, for Ricoeur the differences between the schools can be predicated upon their initial attitude toward the hermeneutic object. Drawing upon his original reflection on the hermeneutic method of the history of religions in *The Symbolism of Evil*, Ricoeur conceived the initial and positive hermeneutic as one which posits an original certitude of the object perceived. In this sense the hermeneutic originating from the history of religions has an "implicit faith" in the object perceived. The outcome of this approach becomes description and not reduction. The sacred object *appears* in the phenomenological sense without a prejudgment of its nature. Ricoeur finds this method to be implicit in Rudolf Otto's discovery of the category of the "holy"; it is developed in the hermeneutic of Mircea Eliade. In Eliade's work this category becomes the category

---

[12] Ricoeur, *De l'interprétation*, p. 36.

of the sacred. Here interpretation is a matter of the recollection of meaning because meaning is discovered and restored by returning to the symbol. Comprehension occurs precisely because one can return to the symbol to discover its meaning as an act of recollection.

For it phenomenolgy is the instrument of listening, of recollection, of restoration of meaning. To believe in order to understand, to understand in order to believe, such is its maxim; and its maxim is the "hermeneutic circle" itself of believing and understanding.[13]

The aim of phenomenology of religion, as well as phenomenology, is this restoration. Correlate with this view is the original thematic statement of Ricoeur, "the symbol invites thought." That principle assumes that the symbol is irreducible and, as such, it induces reflection. It follows from that proposition that the symbol requires immediate belief in its reality.

The alternative is conceived in contrast to this view.

To interpretation as restoration of meaning, we will oppose in the aggregate interpretation according to what I will call collectively the school of suspicion.[14]

In this context interpretation begins by doubting the object. The primary proponents are Marx, Nietzsche, and Freud. Each represents the problem of Cartesian doubt, yet none of the thinkers is finally skeptical. That which separates the three is the distinction made between the false consciousness and the process of deciphering. Freud enters into the problem through the double approach of considering dreams and neurotic symptoms which are deciphered by the economy of drives. For Nietzsche, false consciousness is represented in a critique of cultural value deciphered by the will to power, while the problem for Marx is the appearance of the false consciousness in ideology. The solution to this problem is represented in an economic theory of history and the theory of the class struggle. Ricoeur's argument is that in the context of these thinkers, reflection is directed initially toward a fundamental illusion, a false consciousness which requires a solution in terms of demystification. These positions present the most radical alternative to the phenomenology of the sacred.

At the same time that our three masters of suspicion find their positive convergence, they give to the phenomenology of the sacred and to all hermeneutics conceived as recollection of meaning and remembrance of being, its most radical contrary.[15]

---

[13] Ricoeur, *De l'interprétation*, p. 37.
[14] *Ibid.*, p. 40.
[15] *Ibid.*, p. 43.

This dialectic of hermeneutic types raises the question of freedom and ethics inasmuch as the hermeneutic of suspicion, faced as it is with illusion, raises the question of human bondage to exterior forces. This may be a way of raising the problem of "will" again, but this time in a hermeneutic dialogue. If man is the subject of a determinism, then the major problems of freedom and limitation are raised. Hence, the basic continuity between this discussion and the earlier ones is maintained.

Of course the issue may be raised regarding the extent to which these men are doing a hermeneutic. If one accepts Ricoeur's definition of a hermeneutic as reflection on symbols and language, it seems he has achieved a breakthrough of some importance. The significant step in the transition from *Fallible Man* to *The Symbolism of Evil* was the desire for a concrete encounter with the immediate language of evil. The transition to the later works is predicated on that initial transition. If a global understanding of man requires an encounter with the concrete symbols of experience, then a dialogue with the interpreters of man, culture, and language is necessary. But the dialogue between a hermeneutic which has a recollection of meaning as its foundation and a hermeneutic of suspicion establishes rules and sets the terms for the debate. It is worth noting that the limits of that debate do not end with psychoanalysis. Potentially all the sciences with dual orientations toward man and language can be engaged.

B. PHILOSOPHY AS A REFLECTIVE TASK

Our claim then is that the later writings of Ricoeur represent a growing conviction that a hermeneutic is the methodological subject of philosophy with language as its object. This view of philosophy has enabled Ricoeur to engage in discussion with those among the human sciences whose task it is to render an interpretation of language, a dialogue predicated upon types of interpretation, or a hermeneutic. However, as a consequence it is necessary to define philosophy as a task incorporating the hermeneutic of language. Therefore, philosophy is defined ultimately as a reflective task, a definition that may be understood as a consequence of the proposition "the symbol invites thought." At the heart of that thematic statement is the assumption that philosophy reflects on the symbol.

This definition of philosophy may indicate a departure from Husserl, and this departure may raise questions about the legitimacy of Ricoeur's claim to be ranked as a phenomenologist. However, Ricoeur's departure from Husserl was, we believe, implicit from the outset of *The Philosophy of the Will*. The task of *Freedom and Nature* was to correlate the involuntary with the voluntary inasmuch as the involuntary was only accessible to reflection by an act of mediation. In an earlier chapter it was suggested that Ricoeur was very much part of contemporary French philosophy in his attempt to base philosophy on a concrete foundation. Hence, the phenomenon of the pre-reflexive, as it was represented in Sartre and Merleau-Ponty, is present in Ricoeur from the outset. Initially, Ricoeur's pre-reflexive is found in the involuntary, later in *Fallible Man* it emerges as the hypothesis. *The Symbolism of Evil* states the pre-reflexive more radically in the proposition "the symbol invites thought." In *De l'interprétation* philosophy is defined programmatically as a reflective task. This continuity in Ricoeur's development ought to be recognized; the pre-reflexive in *Freedom and Nature* emerges fifteen years later as the basis for a philosophical program.

But there are those who question Ricoeur's claim to be a phenomenologist particularly after he has suggested a program whereby philosophy is to be concerned with factors of mediation, rather than immediate consciousness. But does not the very definition of philosophy as a task of reflection on language indicate a reliance upon phenomenology? Instead of finding pure consciousness through phenomenological reflection, Ricoeur has found consciousness embedded in language. But it is still the elaboration of consciousness which functions as a directive for his endeavor. Although the battleground for phenomenology may have changed from the criticism of historicism and naturalism, Ricoeur wishes to carry on the same confrontation against behaviorism and the objective systems of language. In this sense, reflective philosophy is equally intent upon developing the means for the recovery of the *Cogito*. Therefore, while Ricoeur has reformulated the phenomenological method, he has done so while retaining its central focus on consciousness and upon the nature of man. To be sure, the method has changed under his endeavors, but with its central intention intact.

The task of this definition of philosophy is informed by Ricoeur's theory of language, which as we have seen is based upon his theory of symbol. In *The Symbolism of Evil*, reflective philosophy does not occur as a definition of the philosophical task. The problematic of that work was made necessary by the overall task of *The Philosophy of the Will*. But that work is a treatise on reflection. The view of philosophy that is implicit in the latter work has been generalized. Again one returns to the thematic statement "the symbol invites thought." Philosophy so conceived constitutes something of a reversal of the philosophical tradition that leads from Descartes through Kant to Husserl. The basic shift inaugurated by a reflective philosophy is from the immediacy of consciousness to the mediation of consciousness.

A reflective philosophy is the opposite of a philosophy of the immediate... We can say somewhat paradoxically, that a reflective philosophy is not a philosophy of consciousness, if by consciousness we understand the immediate consciousness of one's self.[16]

Equally, reflective philosophy is not intuition. From Ricoeur's point of view the self is not given to consciousness, it must be discovered. Consciousness is not a matter of immediacy, it must be revealed inasmuch as reflective philosophy constitutes itself in reflection as an act both existential and ethical.

Such is the ultimate root of our problem: it resides in this primitive connection between the act of existing and the sign we unfold in our works; reflection must become interpretation, because I can not grasp this act of existing except in the signs dispersed in the world.[17]

So conceived, consciousness is only revealed through an existential act in relationship to the sign. Consciousness as a phenomenon is not given a priori; it must be discovered through an existential act of interpretation.

Major objections to this point of view are conceivable. For Ricoeur, three basic criticisms are possible. First, does not this conception of philosophy make philosophy contingent upon cultural productions? Conceived as reflection on language, philosophy may place itself in a contingent position. Second, does not philosophy lose its rigor by turning to the opaque and obscure realms of religious symbols and symbols of the unconscious? Third, is not the task of philosophy to act in the name of coherence and consistency?[18]

The answer to these questions and objections revolves around the anthropological center of Ricoeur's thought. If the essence of philosophy is its ability to make logical statements, then reflective philosophy would be false philosophy. But Ricoeur's claim is that logic, particularly symbolic logic, is not the proper aim of philosophy. If the

---

[16] Ricoeur, De l'interprétation, p. 51.
[17] Ibid., p. 54.
[18] Ibid., pp. 54–55.

term logic may be applied to philosophy, it is as a logic of double meaning.

The justification of hermeneutics can be radical only if one searches in the very nature of reflective thought for the principle of a *logic of the double meaning*, a logic which is complex and not arbitrary, rigorous in its articulations, but irreducible to the linearity of symbolic logic.[19]

Such a logic is not objective and formal: rather it suggests the fundamental human possibilities revealed through its subject matter, an anthropological reference. Logic, so conceived, with its anthropological reference is transcendental, while language itself embodies the transcendental as that which contains both the unity and the ambiguity of experience. In this sense the task of philosophy is to engage in reflection precisely because through such a task human actuality and possibility may be understood. Further, so defined, reflective philosophy is a philosophy of the concrete. The price of abstraction, the option of a formal logic, is the loss of concrete human expression.

This is the argument for a philosophy with a reflective foundation. It is distinguished from philosophy which has symbolic logic as its base, as well as the philosophy which has immediate consciousness as its object. Yet different though it may be from the Descartes-Kant-Husserl tradition, its roots are found in a concern for consciousness and the problems of philosophical anthropology. Hence, while seeking to define a new path for philosophy, the organic roots of Ricoeur's thought may be found in that tradition that originally informed phenomenology. In that sense the traditional objects of phenomenological research are still very much a part of Ricoeur's endeavors.

Consistent with Ricoeur's earlier development, the central focus for the set of issues we have been discussing is man, that is, philosophical anthropology. The consequence of the analysis of Freud is a deepening of the basic principles of Ricoeur's philosophical anthropology under the rubric, the archaeology of the subject. In our discussion thus far we have established the reasons for the debate with Freud as a possibility. It is now necessary to investigate the outcome of that debate. Ricoeur's interpretation of Freud has suggested that psychoanalysis is not simply based on a so-called objective system or economy of drives. Rather, Ricoeur's attempt has been to show that psychoanalysis is based on interpretation. If it is a matter of interpretation, and if psychoanalysis has its basis in language, then it is possible to engage that discipline and its classical foundations in debate. That, in fact, is the task of the ana-

[19] Ricoeur, *De l'interprétation*, p. 56.

lytic section of *De l'interptétation*. It attempts to show that psychoanalysis is not what Freud conceived it to be in his earliest writings, that
is, an objective science. Instead, in the context of his later development, it became an interpretation of the psyche and culture. The analytic section of *De l'interprétation* lays the foundation for the dialogue
with Freud.

Ricoeur, careful not to claim that psychoanalysis is based on philosophical reflection, does not find that difference sufficient to exclude
it from phenomenological consideration. Freud's work was dedicated
to the analysis of the unconscious, while phenomenology is wedded to
problems of consciousness. Yet Ricoeur argues that psychoanalysis
like phenomenology performs a type of archaeological investigation
which can result in preparing the way for phenomenology. Further, if
the task of psychoanalysis is to recapture the unconscious as its object,
then a type of intersubjective relationship results. Phenomenology
has the same kind of task. Hence, the analytic discourse which constitutes the results of a consideration of Freud can issue in a dialogue.
Another way of putting this problem, which leads to a legitimate discussion, is to point out that the two disciplines have common epistemological foundations. In each case the question of the relationship
between perception and understanding is raised.

The phrase "archaeology of the subject" is formulated as a consequence
of Ricoeur's reading of Freud.

> The directive idea that guides me is this: the philosophical place of analytic dis-
> course is defined by the concept of archaeology of the subject.[20]

It is a phrase designed to capture the central motif of the dialogue.
But the phrase is not read out of Freud's works, nor should it be forced
upon him.

> This concept is not Freud's and we propose neither to impose it by force in the
> reading of Freud, nor to find it through cunning in his work. It is a concept that
> I frame in order to understand myself in reading Freud.[21]

So the meaning of the claim that the central notion of Freud is found
in an archaeology requires an examination. In part the task is one of
showing that the central thrust of Freud's work is not established in
an empirical realism, nor in a causally determined construction, but
in interpretation. This is analogous to the claim that in Freud it is
not only the system but also the method that is important.

---

[20] Ricoeur, *De l'interprétation*, p. 407.
[21] *Ibid.*

The reality of the unconscious is not an absolute reality, but relative to the operations which give it meaning.[22]

Ideally, for Ricoeur, system and interpretation ought to be a matter of
mutual and relational importance. Epistemologically, the relation of
the unconscious and the interpretation of the unconscious should be a
matter of intersubjectivity. Interpretively and methodologically the
unconscious ought to be a matter of both diagnosis and therapy.

Freud's works, when analyzed from the perspective of philosophical anthropology, reveal an orientation toward the anterior roots of
human experience In this sense, Freudianism, rather than a positivism,
represents a romantic view of life.

I for my part see in Freudianism a revelation of the archaic, a manifestation of
the always anterior. It is through that that Freudianism keeps its ancient roots
and puts forth ever new roots in a romantic philosophy of life and the unconscious.[23]

The Freudian orientation attempts to understand the archaic experience
as that revealed in the dream. As such, the Freudian enterprise may
be understood as an adventure in anthropology. Freud is concerned to
discover man's "inner" archaic heritage. Through an analysis of dreams
and an associated system of interpretation the probing of the unconscious
can be understood as an archaic device which has as its aim the discovery of a more "total" view of the subject than ordinary analysis of
consciousness can reveal. Even the Freudian interpretation of culture
may be understood under the same categories. Hence, the Freudian
interpretation of religion and art, though distorted, functioned for the
same end.

At the conclusion of *The Philosophy of the Will* Ricoeur refers to a
"solely human freedom," the ultimate discovery of philosophical anthropology. In that case, freedom was limited by the bodily involuntary. Equally, it is through the discovery of the bodily involuntary that
freedom is given its possibility. If freedom is to be real, that is, a solely human freedom, it must consent to the involuntary as the very
possibility of freedom. An analysis of freedom which does not deal with
those factors, it would follow, is false because it makes of the will,
identified as it is with conscious mental process, "a ghost in a machine,"
to borrow a phrase from Gilbert Ryle. That analysis of a solely human
freedom indicates the depth of Ricoeur's concern for an understanding
of man that is truly global. The analysis of the works of Freud func-

[22] Ricoeur, *De l'interprétation*, p. 423.
[23] *Ibid.*, p. 426.

tions equally for an understanding of that global freedom. If the task of man is to understand fully himself, if the philosopher can truly develop a global understanding of man, then the phenomenon of the unconscious cannot be omitted. A study of Freud is legitimate on this basis alone. Hence, it seems fair to conclude that an archaeology of the subject functions to add another, perhaps deeper dimension, to this endeavor. Meaning is the philosophical problem and an archaeology of the subject functions as a heuristic device whereby meaning can be articulated through uncovering the hidden symbols of the unconscious.

However, an archaeology of the subject is not a complete view of the subject, rather it requires as its compliment a teleology of the subject. Ricoeur's final discussion of Freud involves a comparison of his works with those of Hegel wherein the two meet in a movement of desire which is the birth of culture. Although Hegel would seem to be more involved in the construction of a teleology of the subject, there are reasons for suggesting that he is also to be understood as one who constructs an archaeology of the subject. Archaeology is possible in Hegel because consciousness is not an immediate phenomenon, that is, consciousness is discovered through reflection. Therefore, even though consciousness is a matter of processive development in Hegel's thought, there is an archaic and retrogressive aspect to it, for the movement in Hegel's thought is from consciousness to self-consciousness to reason. It is by the discovery of the self in consciousness that archaeology is possible. Similarly, in Freud the self does become aware of the objects of the unconscious through the semantics of desire, desire being an object toward which one projects himself. Hence, even though the work of Freud is retrospective, there is a teleological aspect to it. Ricoeur's argument is that a global anthropology requires the actualization of both dimensions.[24]

This view of man is consistent with the earlier phases of Ricoeur's philosophical anthropology. The task of *Freedom and Nature* was to understand the *Cogito* in relationship to voluntary and involuntary processes. The hypothesis of *Fallible Man* projected evil as a possibility because man was understood as being suspended between the polarities of finite and infinite. Equally, that work construed freedom and evil as the polarity of human experience. *The Symbolism of Evil* carried this process on by finding man's basic polarity in the multivalence of symbol and myth because they represent both crisis and totality. Hence, the double character of a philosophical anthropology which views

---

[24] Ricoeur, *De l'interprétation*, p. 444-75.

the anthropological subject as suspended between archaeology and teleology is the outcome of a program to develop an anthropology, not as an exercise in rationality, but as one which considers the paradoxical and reconciliation. Archaeology and teleology represent Ricoeur's most recent attempt to account for the polarity of human experience.

Secondly, this view carries out the program of investigation into symbolism in the sense that it constitutes an investigation into the second of its three dimensions. The claim of *The Symbolism of Evil* was that the symbol was tri-dimensional: cosmic, oneiric, and poetic – a complete analysis of the symbol calls for the investigation of all three dimensions. *De l'interprétation* represents the second step in that hermeneutic task inasmuch as it represents an investigation into the oneiric dimension of that phenomenon. The fact that symbols have this triple dimension may not be apparent immediately, yet there are examples. The Oedipus myth is perhaps the most obvious illustration. It can be interpreted as the illustration par excellence of the origin of the unconscious, or it may be interpreted as the archetypal image of human destiny. The first interpretation is psychological, while the second is religious. Both are legitimate. Both analyses, however, exclude its most popular interpretation, that is, as one of the best examples of classical Greek poetry and drama. A full interpretation of the symbol requires all three dimensions.

For Ricoeur, this view of the symbol becomes a critical tool when he turns to Freud's interpretation of culture. If, for example, *Totem and Taboo* and *Moses and Monotheism* are regarded as the last word about the symbol and its relationship to religion and culture, then both are something of a false reduction. In both works, only the psychological validity of the symbol is granted. Thus a positive evaluation of Freud may also be a corrective to his attempt to reduce all things to psychological categories. Of course the proposition could be reversed: a religious interpretation of the symbol is as valid as a psychological or a poetic interpretation of the symbol. Ultimately, all three are necessary.

C. STRUCTURALISM AND PHENOMENOLOGY

The hermeneutic definition of philosophy with its linguistic subject matter correlate with a philosophical anthropology emerges in the later writings of Ricoeur in the context of the dialogue with Freud. Continental philosophy, particularly French phenomenology, in contrast to the analytic philosophy of the English speaking world, has begun to engage the technical side of language, namely structuralism. The reasons for this are perhaps twofold. First, when phenomenology began to take the linguistic turn seriously in France it did so by addressing the classical distinctions between language and speech, synchronic and diachronic linguistics.[25] Second, the structural synchronic model employed by the linguists has become a heuristic device for a number of disciplines in France: literary criticism, anthropology, psychology and philosophy. This latter movement has raised a debate over the merits of a philosophical anthropology in contemporary French thought with Claude Levi-Strauss, Jacques Lacan, Michel Foucault and others, who have been influenced by structuralism and who have reacted in various ways against contemporary influences of existentialism and phenomenology. Inasmuch as Ricoeur has involved himself in the philosophy of language, the issue of structural linguistics and structuralism has found its way into his thought. Ricoeur began a serious analysis of the problems of structuralism in the early 1960s, shortly after the publication of *The Symbolism of Evil*.[26] However, his recent consideration of structuralism is perhaps the most complete.

For obvious reasons Ricoeur finds the problem of language to be the unavoidable challenge to contemporary phenomenology. He states the case forcefully:

This detour through the science of language is not something one can choose to make: it is essential to phenomenology today if it is to survive. For the philosophical front is shifting. Merleau-Ponty fought on two fronts: that of reflective philosophy in its rationalist and neo-Kantian version, and that of behaviorist and objectivist psychology. These are not the main issues today, which are rather the very precise and vigorous epistemological models which have made their appearance in linguistics, with Ferdinand de Saussure and Louis Hjelmslev, and have spread to all the human sciences.[27]

He goes on to say:

This type of model, which we need not hesitate to call semiological, for reasons which I shall give shortly, presents such a radical challenge to phenomenology that it may justly be said that phenomenology will not survive unless it can properly reply to this challenge.[28]

---

[25] Maurice Merleau-Ponty, *Signs*, trans. by Richard C. McCleary (Evanston: Northwestern University Press, 1964), pp. 85–97. In a paper delivered in 1951 Merleau-Ponty begins to address the problem of phenomenology of language in the context of linguistics.

[26] Paul Ricoeur, "Symbolique et temporalité," *Ermeneutica E Tradizione* (Roma: Instituto Di Studi Filosofica, 1963), 5–41.

[27] Paul Ricoeur, "New Developments in Phenomenology in France: The Phenomenology of Language." *Social Research*, XXXIV (Spring, 1967), p. 14.

[28] *Ibid.*

The challenge of semiology – more simply of structuralism – is its willingness to opt for objective systems over subjective interpretation. This is a problem for phenomenology, for it represents one more version of the naturalist attitude, an objective determinism.

The ultimate presupposition of any structural linguistics is that language is an object, that is like the subject matter of other sciences, where, also, the "thing" is resolved into a relationship, a system of internal dependencies. For phenomenology, however, language is not an object but a mediation, that is to say, it is that by which and through which we move towards reality (whatever it may be). For phenomenology, language consists in saying something about something: it thereby escapes toward what it says: it goes beyond itself and dissolves in its intentional movements of reference.[29]

Ricoeur traces this difficulty to Hjelmslev's theory that language is nothing more than a system of internal relations, a system of signs with no external reference. As such, interpretation is excluded from consideration. This initial judgment on the part of structural linguistics is dependent upon de Saussure's distinction between language and speech, and his complete separation between the two. It is because of this assumption that language can exist as a universe of signs with no other reference than one of internal relations.

For Ricoeur, the apparent and obvious task of phenomenology of language is the reassessment of the relationship between language and speech. The concern of phenomenology is the relationship between language and the subject. Hence, it cannot eliminate speech. But neither can one reject the findings of linguistics. Therefore, in contrast to previous phenomenologies of language, Ricoeur states:

This reanimated phenomenology cannot be content with repeating the old descriptions of speech which do not recognize the theoretical status of linguistics and its first axiom, the primacy of structure over process. It cannot even rest content with contrasting what it might call the openness of language to the lived world of experience with the closedness of the universe of signs for the linguist. It is through and by means of a linguistics of language that a phenomenology of speech is today conceivable.[30]

There are three ways in which this proposal for a phenomenology of speech and language may be correlated with a structural theory of language, with its conception of languages as a system of signs. The first way is through the incorporation of the phenomenological theory of intentionality into the structural theory of signs. So conceived, language as a system points beyond itself in the sense that the sign

[29] Ricoeur, "New Developments in Phenomenology in France: The Phenomenology of Language." 16.
[30] Ibid., 19.

points to a thing signified, implying that language has an intentional function. There would then be a relationship between the sign and the problem of meaning, inasmuch as the sign as meaning would point beyond the system. The phenomenological interpretation would then be the reactivation of the system of language in terms of meaning. It is then by speech, the intentional referent of the system of signs, that language is reactivated.

Language is mediated through the speaker by means of the sentence. Technically, this is the translation from semiotics to the sentence. As structural linguistics has shown, language may be explained in terms of an internal system of signs, but practically, language functions on the basis of use. Hence, the attempt to activate language for Ricoeur constitutes a kind of Wittgensteinian transition from schema to use. To make the transition from the scheme of signs to the sentence requires a correlate transition from language to speech. This is not to reject the semantic function of language. Rather, this is a way in which the dichotomy between language and speech is overcome.

What phenomenology must do, then is to take up again the theory of meaning and put it to the test of semiology in order to proceed to a genuine dialectic of semiology and semantics at every level of the units of speech.[31]

With this analysis as a foundation, the second task of a phenomenology of language is to address the role of the speaking subject. In order to clarify this role, Ricoeur recalls Husserlian foundations. If, in Husserl, knowledge is a matter of self-constitution, it follows that language as a system of signs is at the disposal of the subject. However, a classical phenomenological analysis does not constitute a technical solution to the problem. This transition from the potentiality of the system of signs to its actualization through the subject can be shown by an analysis of that system of signs as activated by and through the subject. The example used is the function of the signs of the personal pronouns, "I" and "you." Considered by itself in a system of signs without any external referent the sign "I" is simply an empty designation. Considered from the perspective of the subject as the self-constituting reality around which language is invoked it is the basis for the activation of language. Consequently, the task of phenomenology is to understand the subject in the context of language through the subject's centralizing and significatory powers.

---

[31] Ricoeur, "New Developments in Phenomenology in France: The Phenomenology of Language," 23.

The task of phenomenology can now be seen more clearly: this posing itself of the subject, invoked by the whole tradition of the *Cogito*, must now be operated within language and not alongside it, or we shall never get beyond the contradiction between semiology and phenomenology. It must be made to take place in the instance or episode of communication, that is in the act through which the potential system of language becomes the actual occurrence of speech.[32]

The third area in which a phenomenology of language can meet the challenge proposed by structuralism is to rediscover in language the origin of the symbolic function. The prior discussion has established the basic rules for this procedure. To reunite language and speech, the sign and the subject, requires a reappraisal of the relationship between the sign and the thing signified. If it is discovered that this duality and unity is present in language, even within the sign, then the question of its origin is legitimate. It is at this point that the question of the relevance of the phenomenological reduction may be raised. The reduction can solve the enigma of the origin of the dual function of language by discovery of the centrality of the subject and the use of the symbolic function as a way of understanding or of becoming a being-for-meaning. By discovering the origin of meaning in the symbol which is given through the speaking subject, one has again redressed the relationship of language and speech.

We have entered into this discussion of Ricoeur's consideration of structuralism because it represents the most recent development in Ricoeur's program for reflective philosophy directed toward the development of an archaeology of the subject and the development of a phenomenological hermeneutic. For Ricoeur, this debate with structuralism takes on characteristics of "crisis" because structuralism, conceived as a mere system of signs, rules out the centrality of the subject and therefore most of the things he has attempted to establish in *The Philosophy of the Will* and the later writings. The opposition to the view of the centrality of the subject in a structuralist system is considerable. Anthropologist Claude Levi-Strauss, literary critic Roland Barthes, psychoanalyst Jacques Lacan, and philosophers Michel Foucault and Louis Althusser, have all argued for a more or less classical structuralist system at the expense of the subject. Significantly, Ricoeur has not rejected structuralism, but he has seen its neo-positivistic overtones. To that extent the present focus of his thought has been concerned with an attempt to conceive structuralism in the context of the central role of the subject.

---

[32] Ricoeur, "New Developments in Phenomenology in France: The Phenomenology of Language," 27.

But this consideration of structuralism is not simply a matter of protest. It is apparent that the transition from *Fallible Man* to *The Symbolism of Evil* was a transition to language as the subject matter of philosophy. The initial appraisal of language led toward an attempt to develop a total theory of language. Although this theory is not yet complete, the encounter with structuralism represents the continuation of his constructive development.

So we may conclude that the later writings of Ricoeur have tended to concretize the original problem, namely the presentation of a global understanding of man. This has led to a number of interesting developments implicit in the evolution of the first two chapters of our discussion of Ricoeur. A hermeneutic, originally developed to deal with symbols, has become the methodological subject matter of a philosophical program while study of language has become the object of that program. This has made it possible for Ricoeur to engage other disciplines which use and develop special languages. This engagement with other disciplines has made it possible to distinguish between various hermeneutic types. With this given set of problems and solutions, Ricoeur has been able to show the direction of the philosophical task by labeling it a reflection on language, the philosophy of the concrete. As was the case in the earlier discussions, the motivating question for such a view of philosophy is the question, who is man? It was out of this problem and concern that the notion of the archaeology of the subject arose.

D. RICOEUR'S HERMENEUTIC: AN EVALUTION

In this concluding discussion of Ricoeur's work we wish to raise the question of Ricoeur's contribution to hermeneutics in the context of a consideration of central figures in its history, namely Schleiermacher, Otto, and Bultmann. In so doing, we will be returning to the initial problem of this discussion, the correlation between mythic-symbolic language and philosophical anthropology. Equally, we will be evaluating Ricoeur's role in the formulation of that problem. The criterion for the choice of the three figures is that Schleiermacher is the classic interpreter of "religion"; Otto's theory represents one of the first significant most popular statements of a hermeneutic in contemporary thought; while Bultmann's view represents one of the most popular statements of hermeneutics in contemporary experience.

There are two basic factors in Schleiermacher's interpretation: the first is the primordial character of feeling; the second is his conception of a hermeneutic as an art and not as a science. Bultmann correctly claims that that which distinguishes Schleiermacher's hermeneutic theory from earlier hermeneutic discussions was the romantic philosophy of life. This meant a departure from the view that a hermeneutic is simply a matter of the proper application of a set of philosophical rules. Rather, a hermeneutic is a matter of subjective appropriation; a hermeneutic is an art. The aesthetic analysis of religion occurs in his earliest work.

> And yet, however high you go; though you pass from laws to the Universal Lawgiver, in whom is the unity of all things; though you allege that nature cannot be comprehended without God, I would still maintain that religion has nothing to do with knowledge, and that, quite apart from it, its nature can be known.[33]

Rather, knowledge of religion as the object of reflection is a matter of feeling.

> Yet religion is not knowledge and science, either of the world or of God... In itself it is an affection, a revelation of the Infinite in the finite, God being seen in it and it in God.[34]

By this designation of religion as the hermeneutic object, Schleiermacher was attempting to establish and make legitimate a sphere for the much harassed realm of interpretation.

> Only by keeping outside the range both of science and of practice can it maintain its proper sphere and character. Only when piety takes its place along side of science and practice, as a necessary and indispensable third...will the common field be together occupied and human nature in this side be complete.[35]

To designate the object of religious interpretation as neither an object of science nor a formal epistemology means, in Schleiermacher's case, that the true nature of the religious object is "immediate consciousness of the deity as he is found in ourselves and in the world."[36]

The position Schleiermacher developed in his *Speeches* remained relatively consistent throughout his later works. In his monumental work, *The Christian Faith*, feeling is again the central norm for interpretation, that is, feeling as immediate self-consciousness. Inasmuch as feeling is sustained as primary over knowing and doing, the task was to designate the kind of feeling that was religious and interpret Christian doctrine in that context. The doctrine of absolute dependence became

---

[33] Friedrich Schleiermacher, *On Religion: Speeches to its Cultured Despisers* (Harper Torchbook; New York: Harper and Brothers, Publishers, 1958), p. 35.

[34] *Ibid.*, p. 37.

[35] *Ibid.*, pp. 37–38.

[36] *Ibid.*, p. 101.

the central notion. The task of interpretation was to translate all state-ments about God and the world through the primary experience of feeling. From the perspective of interpretation the third and the thir-tieth propositions respectively are the most important propositions of *The Christian Faith*. The first defined self-consciousness as the center of piety, while the second claims that statements about God and the world will be interpreted through it.[37]

Schleiermacher's great contribution to the hermeneutic study was his attempt to rescue interpretation from the field of objective and empirical science. With this task in mind, feeling became the most im-portant subjective category dominating interpretation. Hence, feeling, or immediate self-consciousness, could be said to be the hermeneutic tool whereby all religious forms could be interpreted. In the field of hermeneutic analysis this position represents the first acknowledgment of the intersubjective relationship between interpreter and object interpreted. Equally, it points to the historical character of human un-derstanding.

But if Schleiermacher may be credited with having established the modern character of a hermeneutic, one of his interpreters, Rudolf Otto, chose to criticize him for, in a sense, not making his hermeneutic position radical enough. Otto states:

His mistake is making the distinction merely that between "absolute" and "re-lative" dependence, and therefore a difference of degree and not of intrinsic quality.[38]

Otto wanted to establish the absolute independence of the object of religious interpretation. Otto found it necessary to depart from Schleier-macher because he felt Schleiermacher simply failed to give full cre-dence to the independence of the religious object. Therefore, Otto's most stinging criticism of Schleiermacher was the suggestion that his religious category was simply emotional.

The religious category discovered by him by whose means he professes to deter-mine the real content of religious emotion, is merely a category of *self*-salvation, in the sense of self-depreciation.[39]

For Otto, Schleiermacher represented a type of reductionism of the religious object to a matter of feeling. Otto attempted to get behind this limitation by pointing to the "irrational" character of the religious object. Charles H. Long has made Otto's position clear:

[37] Friedrich Schleiermacher, *The Christian Faith* (Edinburgh: T and T Clark, 1928), pp. 5, 125.
[38] Rudolf Otto, *The Idea of the Holy* (New York: Oxford University Press, 1958), p. 9.
[39] *Ibid.*, p. 10.

The watershed of phenomenological studies...is represented by Rudolf Otto's *The Idea of the Holy*. Otto attacks the problem head on by describing the a priori religious category of the consciousness. Religious expressions and their peculiar modalities are manifestations of a *sui generis* religious consciousness.[40]

Rudolf Otto represents a real advance over Schleiermacher, for he attempted to show that the object of a hermeneutic is something more than historical experience; it has an a priori character, a character that, even though it is a part of feeling, cannot be reduced to feeling.

It is to Rudolf Bultmann's credit that he was the first to introduce the problem of the object of interpretation as a problem for language. Although we have already suggested the major difficulties presented by Bultmann's proposal and the problems to which it has led in terms of contemporary interpretation of religion, in this context the significant advance of Bultmann over the earlier figures was the realization that the object of a hermeneutic of religion is myth. Hence, Bultmann's contribution to this discussion has been to make hermeneutics a problem for language. But this does not eliminate our earlier criticism. Bultmann's mistake was to argue for the elimination of myth on the basis of an anthropology which presupposed an historical-evolutionary hypothesis.

In a sense Ricoeur's position on the hermeneutic of language contains a strain of all the previous hermeneutic positions. With Schleiermacher he shares the belief that a hermeneutic can be sustained only through the recovery of the subject as interpreter. He would agree that hermeneutics is therefore a matter of consciousness. With Otto, however, he would find the proper definition of the task of a hermeneutic in the description of its object as a phenomenon that is not reducible. If the object of a hermeneutic is somewhat different for Ricoeur, in the sense that it is not simply "wholly other," but a symbol, agreement would be sustained on the basis of the claim that the object is irreducible. Finally, he would agree with Bultmann that the proper object of a hermeneutic is language.

But the real significance of Ricoeur's hermeneutic position is its distinctiveness from the others. First, it represents an advance over Schleiermacher's position inasmuch as it shows that a hermeneutic is not a problem of immediate self-consciousness, but a problem for language. For Ricoeur, therefore, the phenomenon of immediate self-consciousness is a misnomer. Consciousness is mediated through its subject.

---

[40] Charles H. Long, "Archaism and Hermeneutics," *The History of Religions*, Vol. I *Essays on the Problem of Understanding* (Chicago and London: The University of Chicago Press, 1967), p. 69.

More important, Ricoeur has moved beyond the unspecifiability of feeling to the specifiable realm of language to designate the object of a hermeneutic. If feeling is not the sole object of a hermeneutic, it is not denied therefore; feeling is present in language. This is not to depreciate the work of Schleiermacher. It was Schleiermacher after all who laid the foundations for the modern problem of a hermeneutic by emphasizing the centrality of the subject in the hermeneutic process.

From the perspective of Ricoeur's contribution, the significant innovation was given by Rudolf Otto. Otto's claim that the religious object is "wholly other" is correlate to Ricoeur's claim that "the symbol invites thought" in the sense that the object of interpretation is irreducible. But Ricoeur's objection to Otto would be that it is not enough to designate the object of interpretation as an irreducible phenomenon; it is necessary to show how the symbol does inform thought. In Ricoeur's case that designation develops into a theory of symbol and finally into a theory of language. Finally, Ricoeur's position with regard to Bultmann should be apparent. Although he accepts the position that the hermeneutics of religion is a matter of the hermeneutics of symbol and myth, he definitely does not accept the position that hermeneutics is a matter of reduction.

E. CONCLUSION

As a consequence of this study of the later writings of Ricoeur, it is possible to expand the proposition which concluded the last chapter. If philosophical anthropology requires a consideration of mythic-symbolic language as a correlate dimension, this view has now been given a broader linguistic and anthropological context, inclusive of the investigation into psychological symbols and structural linguistics. With regard to the argument of this essay two problems arise. Does this development mitigate against the necessary inclusion of mythic-symbolic language? Further, regardless of the answer to that question, what is added to the consideration of mythic-symbolic language by those recent ventures?

We believe that Ricoeur's recent adventure in hermeneutic theory and language does not negate the original proposition, but in fact it adds an important dimension to it. Ricoeur's investigation of symbols was predicated originally upon a very restricted consideration of religious symbols as a contributory phenomenon to global anthropology

The context for the discussion was set by the problems presented in *The Philosophy of the Will*. But this approach, unique and distinctive though it was, raised a number of unanswered questions. What is the relationship of the religious symbol to other types of discourse? Can one have a theory of symbol without setting it in the context of a theory of language? Is a hermeneutic restricted to the interpretation of symbols alone? At the conclusion of *The Symbolism of Evil* the reader was left with the provocative, but not fully specified theme, "the symbol invites thought." It was not yet clear that the principles developed in that work would become the basis for an entire philosophical position. It is evident that in the later writings these principles have become the basis for an entire philosophical position.

Rather than mitigate against the proposition that a mythic-symbolic language is necessary for a full understanding of man, these developments can only enhance that proposition. There are reasons for this suggestion. First, a consideration of mythic-symbolic language is isolated unless it is placed in the context of a total theory of language. It would be absurd to claim that mythic-symbolic language functions in terms of cannons germane solely to itself. Therefore, it is necessary to show that the validity of mythic-symbolic discourse may be justified in the context of a general theory of discourse. Second, a global anthropology cannot be sustained simply on the basis of an analysis of religious symbols and myths. To call such an anthropology global would be a contradiction in terms. The interpretation of Freud and the dialogue with structuralism present another dimension of that task. Third, in both instances the broader context of interpretation can only function for the necessary consideration of mythic-symbolic language.

Given the set of the critical problems raised in the first chapter of this essay, namely the types of hermeneutic theory which eliminate mythic-symbolic discourse on the assumption that man no longer requires such primary forms, these late developments of Ricoeur show why such a position need not be taken.

However, we should not like to claim that the task of setting the full scope for language and anthropology has been completed by Ricoeur. Rather, Ricoeur has laid a new foundation for the correlation between mythic-symbolic language and philosophical anthropology. In the concluding chapter we wish to construct from that foundation by developing a theoretical and methodological alternative to the problem of a negative correlation between mythic-symbolic language and philosophical anthropology presented at the outset of this essay.

V

TOWARD A WORKING THEORY OF LANGUAGE CORRELATED WITH A PHILOSOPHICAL ANTHROPOLOGY

Ricoeur's distinctive mode of philosophizing may capture the imagination of a philosophical generation. Its significance will depend upon the person who examines it. To the phenomenologist, the significance of Ricoeur's thought will be found in his revision of the phenomenological method. To the analytic thinker, the measure of Ricoeur's work may be in his plunge into an analysis of language. The structuralist may find the significance of Ricoeur's thought in his attempt to reconsider the relationship of language and speech. The hermeneut may find the measure of Ricoeur's achievement in his attempt to incorporate a hermeneutic into a philosophical program. To those who are interested in myth and symbolism, the significance of Ricoeur's thought may be found in his distinctive mode of interpretation of that primary phenomenon. As the introduction of this essay stated, Ricoeur's thought, like the symbol, is multivalent. Our analysis simply has attempted to bring these multivalent themes together and thereby to understand its unity and direction.

This final chapter is conceived as a response to the thought of Paul Ricoeur. As stated in the introduction, such a task is not an attempt to think beyond our subject, but to do one's own thinking in response to Ricoeur's thought.

Ricoeur's significance can be measured in terms of the problems he has attempted to solve. Is mythic-symbolic language simply a "primitive" mode of discourse which has been transcended by our "modern" epoch, or does it have a special intention? In a sense that is the question. Does a hermeneutic procedure require a reductionistic motif, or are there other alternatives? Our analysis would seem to suggest that mythic-symbolic language provides a level of meaning otherwise unattainable. Therefore, it seems possible to suggest that a positive correlation between mythic-symbolic language and philosophical anthropology can be constructed. Constructive speculations will be confined to the philosophy of religion (the traditional domain of mythic-symbolic language) and philosophical anthropology.

Therefore, the purpose of this concluding chapter is to present our correlation between mythic symbolic language and philosophical anthropology as a constructive alternative to arguments which have placed less stress upon primary mythic-symbolic forms and more stress upon a rather restricted definition of modernity. A theory of mythic-symbolic language does not have to begin with the assumption that primary symbolic forms are invalid. It does not have to assume that modernity is juxtaposed to myth. The thought of Ricoeur sustains that thesis.

Let us turn then from criticism and analysis to construction. The basis for the development of a constructive alternative is provided by our prior analysis. We will place these findings in a methodological context appropriate to philosophy of religion, free from an etiological definition of primary religious forms and the juxtaposition of myth and modernity.

A distinction between theory and method is required to provide a constructive foundation for the linguistic and anthropological poles of this position. Theory, given this context, refers to foundation. Method refers to the manner in which this theoretical position can be developed. In this case theory makes method possible. The theory that occurs in this discussion is predicated on the concrete investigation that preceded it. On the theoretical side investigations into mythic-symbolic language require: (1) an elaboration of a hermeneutical orientation informed by the thought of Ricoeur, (2) a consideration of the definition of myth and symbol, and (3) the elaboration of this view of language in a general theory of language.

The manner in which one treats language is affected by implicit assumptions about the nature of man. Therefore the reciprocity between mythic-symbolic language and philosophical anthropology can, and must, be established. Prior to the establishment of a theory of language, it is necessary to free myth from juxtaposition to modernity, to circumvent the distinction between a logical and a pre-logical mentality. This anthropological problem requires "first order" consideration because only on the basis of different anthropological assumptions can a different theory of language be developed. As we shall try to show, this orientation requires the incorporation of a phenomenological epistemology basically Husserlian in character.

The first theoretical step on the anthropological side will be followed by a second theoretical step pertaining to language. Based on a phenomenological model the theory of language will be composed of three parts: (1) hermeneutics, (2) definition, and (3) a consideration of mythic-symbolic language in the context of language. After a theory of language has been established, it will be possible to turn again to anthropological considerations by specifying the significance of mythic-symbolic language in the context of a philosophical anthropology. This latter step will allow the specification of the uniqueness of mythic-symbolic language as well as show why mythic-symbolic language has a necessary anthropological function.

In establishing this two-fold theoretical foundation the following factors are at work: (1) the limitations revealed at the critical juncture of this essay, (2) the contributions of Ricoeur to the theoretical issues raised, and (3) the phenomenological context which informs and influences the entire position. The theoretical discussion will establish the positive correlation between mythic-symbolic language and a philosophical anthropology sought at the outset of this essay.

The transition from the theoretical to the methodological constitutes a shift in emphasis from the problem of grounding a position to problems of application. The methodological consequences of this theoretical position can be developed in the philosophy of religion. By philosophy of religion, a rather schematic definition is intended: reflection upon religion as constituted by a multiplicity of linguistic forms. Reflection of the philosophical kind, informed as it is by phenomenology, is concerned with the meaning of the multiplicity of religious phenomena. This transition from theory to method is necessary for two reasons: (1) to develop the consequences of theory, and (2) to show that this position, when driven to its methodological form can circumvent the problems referred to in the first chapter.

A. THEORY

1. Phenomenological Epistemology and the Possibility of a New Anthropological Model

In this discussion the original correlation between mythic-symbolic language and philosophical anthropology was fundamentally negative. That correlation was limited by the definition of primary religious language and also by the understanding of man upon which it was predicated. Ricoeur rejects the kinds of anthropological assumptions that would result in the depreciation of the primary religious forms, that is, myth and symbol.[1] In the first chapter of this discussion reference was made to the negative assumption which supported an etiological view of myth, namely the historical-evolutionary hypothesis. Such a view of mythic-symbolic forms assumes that there is a radical cleavage between a pre-modern and a modern age. One is mythic and the other is scientific, for inasmuch as myth is in part a primitive science, it is surpassed by the explanations of modern science because the latter offer a better and more complete explanation.

Provision for a more positive rendering of primary mythic-symbolic language requires the avoidance of the historical-evolutionary hypothesis or model. Therefore it is necessary to provide the theoretical framework which will yield a more adequate understanding of man. The proper theoretical framework for a philosophical anthropology which will lead to a positive evaluation of mythic-symbolic language can be provided by a phenomenological epistemology grounded in Husserl's thought.

Although the phenomenological method is often called a method of description, a more adequate way of stating the central theme of phenomenology is to define it as a skeptical method which applies radical doubt in order to achieve apodicticity. That is what is meant by Husserl's notion of "rigorous science,"[2] namely the attempt to found philosophy on certitude. Husserl, like Kant, accepted Hume's criticism that science could not be founded on any objective certitude. At the same time he argued that the transcendental method was able to recover a certitude which would enable it to provide the foundation for a new philosophy. Husserl was in agreement with Kant's philosophical restatement of the Copernican revolution. Knowledge is a matter of self-constitution. The epistemological consequence of this revolution was that instead of assuming that knowledge occurs through the influence of objects upon the mind (Locke and Hume), Kant theorized

[1] We have seen how the assumption that modern man is somehow beyond the realm of primary mythic-symbolic forms has been an initial problem. With Ricoeur it was the positive evaluation of symbolic forms plus the desire to see mythic-symbolic language as a necessary contribution to a global anthropology that allowed freedom from the difficulties presented by etiological definitions and associated anthropological assumptions. Assumptions about a distinction between the modern and the pre-modern were rejected and the way was opened for a positive correlation.

[2] Edmund Husserl, "Philosophy as Rigorous Science," *Phenomenology and the Crisis of Philosophy*, trans. by Quentin Lauer (Harper Torchbook; New York, Evanston, London: Harper and Row, Publishers, 1965), pp. 71–147.

that the self is engaged actively in the process of making up knowledge. Husserl concluded from this basic insight that the certitude for which philosophy seeks can in no sense be drawn from an analysis of the so-called objective world. Instead certitude can be discovered through a transcendental analysis of the *ego Cogito*. This insight provided the basis for his admiration of Descartes, whose method of absolute doubt led to the self as the *indubitandum*, the apodictic, the *Cogito, ergo sum*.

Husserl holds in common with Kant and Descartes the understanding that the self provides the constitutive basis for knowledge in the sense that whatever we know is in fact grounded in the apodictic ego.[3] Husserl sought to explore that epistemological ground for knowledge, uncovering "noetic" and "noematic" structures which underlie the experience of the ego. On the basis of the discovery that the self provides the constitutive foundation for all knowledge, Husserl carried on a lifelong battle with what he called the "natural attitude." The "natural attitude" was present most specifically in naturalistic psychology and naturalism, but it was also apparent in any approach that attempted to establish itself on the assumption that knowledge is somehow objective.

One conclusion can be drawn from this epistemological orientation, which, although Husserl was never fully aware of it, is implicit in his position. Earlier the claim was made that Bultmann required an historical-evolutionary hypothesis for understanding man. In contrast, the underlying model assumed at this juncture is one which affirms the primacy of consciousness. Since consciousness becomes the defining factor for knowledge, the phenomenological problem is to discover what is constitutive for consciousness per se. It was this fact that led Husserl to postulate a theory of regions to account for the various manifestations of consciousness.

On the basis of this "Husserlian" mode of thought, consciousness manifests itself in a number of simultaneous dimensions at any particular time. This does not mean that history and evolution are to be excluded from this view. History is every particular man's creation. The constant factor in history is the existence of the self, the *Cogito*. Man creates time, time is not objectively given. It is this valuation, the valuation of the centrality of the ego, that remains constant and is not relative. By this approach Husserl thought he had transcended the difficulties of historicism. The abiding factor, that upon which

---

[3] Edmund Husserl, *Cartesian Meditations*, trans. by Dorion Cairns (The Hague: Martinus Nijhoff, 1960), p. 36.

philosophy could base itself in all historical periods, is the apodictic ego. Man in no age could be said to be relative to the sum of its products and ideas presented in a so-called *Weltanschauung*.[4] As a consequence, it is not possible to reject the products of man's past as things now irrelevant on the basis of contemporary experience. Since man expresses himself fully in his cultural productions in every age, these phenomena are constitutive for his full global expression.

Husserl's discovery may be regarded as revolutionary because of its assumptions about the nature of consciousness. More important for the subject under discussion is its implication for primary mythic-symbolic language. From this perspective it is possible to regard the distinctive products of man's conscious experience, not in juxtaposition to one another, but in correlation with the various levels of consciousness. One does not have to juxtapose a mythic age to a scientific one. Myth, as the human linguistic expression of the sacred, and science, as a mode of knowing which enables man to derive a technology to help him survive, are legitimate dimensions of man's conscious experience. Each has an equal validity and a positive value. It may be assumed that both are necessary for a global understanding of man.

2. Hermeneutics: The Initial Validity of the Mythic-Symbolic Form

The Husserlian "consciousness" model provides an epistemological basis for an alternative understanding of man. It provides part of the solution to the problem of interpreting primary mythic-symbolic forms by dissolving the distinction between the logical and the prelogical, that is, the juxtaposition between myth and modernity. This step, significant though it may be, does not solve the problem. Husserl provides us with neither an interpretation of the function of language nor the hermeneutical tools for understanding it.

The first linguistic problem that must be overcome is the construction of a hermeneutic which will grant initial validity to mythic-symbolic language dispensing with any negative pre-judgment of myth and symbol. As Husserlian epistemology allows us to dispense with a negative pre-judgment concerning the nature of man, so it is necessary to dispense with similar judgments with regard to the nature of language. That such an orientation is possible is part of the initial burden of the hermeneutic of Paul Ricoeur.

---

[4] In one of his earliest essays, Husserl spoke directly to this problem in his criticism of *Weltanschauung* philosophy. Husserl, *Phenomenology and the Crisis of Philosophy*, pp. 122–47.

The most important factor in the construction of a hermeneutic is the starting point. If one assumes that the primary forms are of questionable validity, the manner in which one understands these forms will be affected. In this sense the kind of anthropological theory that informs the hermeneutic starting point is crucial. In fashioning a hermeneutic, Ricoeur has approached mythic-symbolic phenomena from a phenomenological perspective in the sense just indicated. The primary assumption is one which leads to inquiry about the role of such phenomena as a constitutive factor for consciousness. Since symbols and myths contribute to consciousness as such, the immediate problem is one of understanding them as a dimension of human experience.

Ricoeur's concern to approach the symbols and the myths of evil, to understand man's concrete encounter with evil in the language of avowal, supports the same interpretation. The assumption is that mythic-symbolic phenomena can contribute to a dimension of experience.[5] If one were to diminish the initial validity of the mythic-symbolic form, one would fail to grasp that form at its own level.

For Ricoeur an initial hermeneutic judgment is operative which is carried into the realm of philosophical reflection. The thinker does not think through the symbol, nor behind the symbol, but from the symbol. "The symbol invites thought." People with a philosophic interest in religion have tried often to correlate mythic-symbolic forms with a philosophic ontology. The framework for the interpretation of symbol and myth is already given by the philosophic system. Ricoeur's hermeneutic alternative constitutes a reversal of that approach. From his perspective it is the symbol that informs meaning; meaning is not imposed upon the symbol. The symbol becomes the informative factor determining philosophical reflection. This reversal of a traditional methodology places the symbol and myth in a light totally different from that which was assumed previously.

---

[5] In terms of the original criticism contained in this discussion, is not this the very thing that Bultmann and the secular, God is dead, religious thinkers do? Do they not desire an existential interpretation of myth which would support this desire for an anthropological dimension? The similarity is obvious but superficial. In their case the existential interpretation occurs at the expense of the original mythic-symbolic form. The form is judged to be an inadequate false modality which intends another thing than it expresses. However, from this phenomenological perspective, it is the form itself that is important. The problem in the case of the former is to find a means of incorporating this phenomenon into modern consciousness. In the case of the latter, it is the form itself which is affirmed. In Ricoeur's case one turns to the form of symbol and myth to uncover consciousness. In terms of the phenomenological alternative the only judgment that is made about the mythic-symbolic form is that the form can contribute to consciousness because it constitutes a dimension of human experience.

3. Mythic-Symbolic Language and the Problem of Definition

The first chapter of this essay illustrated the difficulties present in the construction of a correlation between myth, etiologically defined, and man. It is logical to assume that a different hypothesis about man will yield a different definition of mythic-symbolic language. The Husserlian "consciousness" model makes such a definition possible. The Husserlian consciousness model also allows for the development of criteria that can be used in the definition of primary mythic-symbolic language. We stated that the historical-evolutionary hypothesis results in an etiological definition of myth. This definition has three negative consequences: (1) it raises the question of the validity of primary mythic-symbolic language, (2) it tends to associate that primary language with a particular period in human history, and (3) this association is complemented by an "evolutionary" view which tends to base a mythic-symbolic heritage on the ideal of the historical evolution of consciousness.

The possibility of the Husserlian model is that none of these negative assumptions needs to be incorporated. The result is a distinctive turn from the negative to the positive. Primary language (particularly myth) is not a species of spurious and improper language. Myth, as a representation of a specific region of consciousness, is valid. Second, myth is not a species of a particular age: myth is a product of human experience per se. Third, since the production of myth can be found in all ages of human life, an evolutionary hypothesis is irrelevant to the discussion. Consequently, the way is opened for a much more affirmative definition of mythic-symbolic language. At this point the anthropological model and the hermeneutic foundation are complementary.

4. Definition: The Validity of Mythic-Symbolic Language

On the basis of these epistemological and hermeneutical foundations we seek a theoretical basis for a definition of mythic-symbolic language. In order to arrive at this definition it is first necessary to consider the claims of that language. We believe that the intrinsic claim of mythic-symbolic language is the claim to be a valid language. Of course, the issue of validity is at the heart of the discussion of an interpretation of mythic-symbolic language. Because symbols and myths were thought to be invalid a hermeneutic of reduction arose. It is against this view that Ricoeur's theory and analysis of symbol and myth are presented. Validity may be the claim of all types of language. In order to solve the problem of the validity of scientific language the issue of verification or falsification is raised inasmuch as a scientific language is valid when it can be verified or falsified. In a similar way, religious language sustains a claim to validity, but its validity is apparent only when intrinsic and special characteristics are perceived.

The term "validity" has a double meaning. Analyzed in relation to claim and definition, validity implies the potential character of a particular discourse. In this abstract sense validity refers to the possible meaningfulness of mythic-symbolic language in general. The second meaning of validity is concrete. In this context validity refers to the verifiability of a particular set of symbols, for example, the symbols of evil. The first meaning is necessary for a theoretical discussion of mythic-symbolic language because, unless this claim for validity is understood and grounded, a false reductionism of the language is inevitable. As a consequence, once this abstract meaning of validity is established it will be possible to juxtapose this definition of mythic-symbolic language to those which share the initial assumption that myth and symbol are invalid. After the abstract meaning of the validity of mythic-symbolic discourse has been established, it will be possible to discuss validity in relationship to problems of verification.

It is possible to begin with a rather broad proposition: *mythic-symbolic language sustains an intrinsic claim to validity*. The proposition can be concretized in three very distinct ways through three subordinate claims: (1) mythic-symbolic language claims uniqueness, (2) mythic-symbolic language claims to represent a specific dimension of experience, and (3) mythic-symbolic language claims to be constitutive for meaning.

Now, these claims inform the definition of mythic-symbolic language in the sense that, understood properly, mythic-symbolic language finally need not be eliminated to be interpreted. By taking into account the claims of mythic-symbolic language for validity, it should be possible to arrive at a theoretical definition which includes validity as a primary category.

a. Uniqueness. Uniqueness means that the primary mythic-symbolic form is distinctive and not replaceable. It has a particular function which is not interchangeable with other forms. This major reversal of definition has consequences for the theories of symbol and myth developed by Ricoeur. This initial assumption allows the development of Ricoeur's theory of symbol and myth because the designation of the significatory power of the symbol indicates its distinctiveness. The symbol is defined first as a sign and as an experience of the world, a designation which points to the specific unique form that the symbol takes.[6]

Inasmuch as many things are modalities of the real, a further specification of the uniqueness of the symbol is required. As we have seen, the uniqueness of the symbol is that its intentionality is not single, but double. Separated from other forms of philosophical thought, the symbol is distinguished by its non-transparent depth character, being composed of a literal and a symbolic intention, the literal intention constituted by the symbolic intention. The example, of course, was illustrated by the dual intention of the symbols of stain, sin, and guilt. The symbol of stain is literally a spot. But built upon this literal intentionality is another intentionality which designates the stain as the situation of defilement of man before the sacred, a second intentionality. It is this multivalence that constitutes the uniqueness of the symbol. Other aspects of Ricoeur's definition point to uniqueness. By revealing a modality of the real (the sacred), the symbol is religious. The uniqueness of the symbol is found in its capacity to reveal paradoxical situations, in the sense that it brings opposites together that can be brought together in no other way. In Ricoeur's thought symbol is distinguished from allegory and the mono-dimensional sign.

Generally, myth may be regarded as a secondary elaboration, a hermeneutic of symbols. Its uniqueness can be explained on several levels. The negative conviction is that an etiological definition of myth is a false interpretation of myth because in Ricoeur's terms it turns myth into gnosis. On the positive side of the issue, the uniqueness of myth is its capacity to narrate a sacred history which serves the interpreters of myth with an explanation of life in terms of sacred events. Beyond that, myth is understood as unique because it provides archetypes or models for action. The distinctiveness of myth may be understood in relationship to human creativity, because myth provides archetypes which can be repeated. Hence, its creative form allows for the development of patterns of action and activity.

Myth can be defined as a unique form. (1) Myth is unique in terms of the sacred history in which it wishes to place the story of man. (2)

---

[6] Paul Ricoeur, *The Symbolism of Evil* trans. by Emerson Buchanan (New York, Evanston, & London: Harper & Row), 1967.

Myth is distinctive in its presentation of models for human action and activity. (3) Myth is unique in its claim to satisfy the quest for origins.

b. Dimension of Experience. Co-extensive with the claim to validity is the claim of the mythic-symbolic form to represent a dimension of experience. Stated phenomenologically and placed within a Husserlian context, this means that myth and symbol represent a region of experience. It also suggests that the so-called existential level of mythic-symbolic modality is not a matter of re-interpretation, because the existential level is given with the mythic-symbolic modality itself. As a consequence if the existential aspect of the mythic-symbolic form is part of the very definition of that modality, it is not necessary to reject that form to interpret and state its existential intention.

Because of their situational and historic origin, both the symbol and the myth may be defined as representative of a level of experience. The symbol and the myth are the result of an occasion or occasions, distinguished by the particularities of time and space. This clarifies the experiential basis of a particular mythic-symbolic form, but it does not specify its distinctive role as a dimension of experience.

Symbols and myths perceived from the experiential side are constitutive for the human quest for totality. The symbol can be distinguished by its attempt to designate a mode of being separated from the concept by its multivalence. Myth is distinctive in its attempt to construe a sacred history, as well as by its presentation of an archetype which can be imitated and repeated. If these two assumptions hold true, then the human quest for totality is found at each level of definition.

The symbol, as referent to a dimension of experience, is distinctive in its ability to bring together and combine opposites; to open possibilities for experiencing that are not ordinarily available. This dimension of experience is unique because of its distinctive role of combination and unification. Therefore, it is in the symbol that the human quest for totality reveals itself.

Myth, on the existential level, may be understood as the product of unhappy consciousness. If myth is part of the quest for totality, the fact that there is a need for that experience, is, in some sense, the reason for it.[7] Myth is an aspect of creativity. The modes of action revealed by myth can be distinguished from ordinary experience by their quest for the extraordinary. They express man's desire to solve enig-

[7] Ricoeur, *The Symbolism of Evil*, p. 167.

mas and riddles of existence. Myth, as symbol, can be understood to represent uniquely a dimension of experience.

c. Meaning. The third aspect of the definition of the mythic-symbolic form involves its claim to be meaningful. This claim is important for at least two reasons, first, because of ordinary identification of myth with falsity, and second, because of the relationship between validity and meaning. If the claim to validity of the primary religious form can be sustained, then the old associations between myth and falsity are no longer tenable. If a form has a basic claim to validity, then it can no longer be dismissed as false.

In terms of the definition developed thus far, we can assume: (1) a mythic-symbolic form has a claim to be meaningful insofar as it represents a unique expression; (2) a mythic-symbolic form can claim meaning in relation to its representation of a particular dimension of experience. To establish this claim, an entirely different criterion for verification than that of etiological definition has been chosen. Rather than impose a definition of modernity which then functions as a principle of verification, verification is derived on the basis of principles more germane to the form itself.

The question of the meaning of the mythic-symbolic forms should be debated on two levels. The first level relates to the meaning value of the form itself while the second level relates meaning as a constitutive factor for belief. The first level is most important for a non-etiological definition of myth. If a mythic-symbolic form can claim validity on the basis of its claim to uniqueness and in terms of its claim to represent a realm of experience, then it is meaningful. At this level of the definition of the mythic-symbolic form, meaning is relevant to the problem of understanding and not to the problem of belief. The meaning value of the mythic-symbolic phenomenon for the interpreter of that form is descriptive initially and not existentially. In the former sense, it is a valid and meaningful form which contributed to our understanding of man's cultural and religious experience. Myths and symbols, as products of particular cultures, have, like art and poetry, an initial meaning value simply as expressions of human experience within that culture. The claim to validity of a mythic-symbolic form bears within it the claim to meaning.

On the level of belief, the question of meaning plays a strikingly different role. At this juncture the individual is asking which, among the multiple myths, is true and meaningful for him. He wants to know which set of symbols is valid for his experience.

Finally, in contradistinction to the etiological definition of mythic-symbolic language, an alternative can be presented. Mythic-symbolic language can be defined as valid because it incorporates a claim to uniqueness, a claim to represent a dimension of experience and a claim to meaning at this basic level of interpretation.

Mythic-symbolic language can be established as a valid language by reference to initial hermeneutic and epistemological assumptions and by definition. Now it is necessary to show how such language can be interpreted.

The construction of an alternative to the reductionistic approach to the problem of meaning involves a view of history and an understanding of symbol and myth. In terms of history, a sacred form always reveals itself in a particular time and space. Further, a mythic-symbolic form may have a history in the sense that it may change and develop in linear time. Yet neither view of history is adequate to explain the meaning of this phenomenon. For every historical manifestation of the sacred there may be other similar hierophanies that appear at different times and places with no historical connection in the sense of historical influence of one form upon the other. Mythic-symbolic facts may be seen best in terms of their structural associations such as their structural commonality and their morphological continuity.

Associated with this view is the assumption that mythic-symbolic language is of such a nature that it can be delineated morphologically and related structurally. The old "battle of myths" with the ultimate claim to the truth of every particular myth is negated by illuminating common structures. A symbol may be integrated into a system because it has a structure. Symbols with common structures are understood fully when they are placed in their proper system.

The consequence of this orientation to symbols is related to the original point of inquiry. First, mythic-symbolic forms are not negated but affirmed. The meaning of the phenomenon is discovered by integrating the form into the system of which it is a part. Discursive structures used to achieve understanding are taken almost directly from the primary symbols.

Ricoeur is neither a morphologist nor a structuralist per se but to the extent that he has employed a comparative method to understand the symbolism of evil, he is necessarily involved in this process. The symbols of stain, sin, and guilt are understood in terms of their particular

meanings and also they constitute an entire symbolism.[8] At the level
of movement from the initial disclosure of a mythic-symbolic form to
the level of its meaning, Ricoeur has developed a hermeneutic which
frees interpretation from the problems of reductionism. The accomplishment of this approach is two-fold: first, the development of an initial
positive evaluation of mythic-symbolic language, and second, a means
of approaching the meaning of this language without reductionism.

5. Mythic-Symbolic Language and the Theory of Language

The discussion of language has been in large part theoretical.
The attempt has been to construct a theory of language which may
be launched as a counteroffensive to the etiological reductionist orientation. The predominant theme has been centered upon validity and
meaning. Our concern has been to show how such language can be
affirmed, understood and interpreted as valid. Rejection of an historical-evolutionary hypothesis about man, acceptance of the Husserlian
consciousness model, a hermeneutic starting point, a definition of the
mythic-symbolic form and finally a structural morphological approach
to the problem of meaning go together to provide the theoretical basis
for the delineation of mythic-symbolic language as meaningful and
valid. One final problem pertaining to the theory of mythic-symbolic
language remains. It is necessary to place the theory of mythic-symbolic language in the context of a theory of language generally.

When Husserl had established the apodictic ego as the foundation for
philosophy as a "rigorous science," he attempted to clarify egological
experience by ascribing regions of noetic-nomatic experience. While the
fruitfulness of this model has already been demonstrated, its implications can be demonstrated now for a theory of language. Husserl failed
to see the significance of a philosophical consideration of language
and instead tried to approach transcendental consciousness per se.
More recent phenomenologists have tended to move beyond Husserl's
reflections on consciousness to a consideration of language as the basis
for and the origin of the reflective process. In keeping with the intention
of the Husserlian orientation, yet bearing in mind the movement of
phenomenology toward language, the possibility of a *regional* theory
of language can be presented. Such a theory of language assumes that
instead of describing regions of conscious experience, they are regions
of conscious experience reflected in language. By this investigation

---

[8] Ricoeur, *The Symbolism of Evil*, p. 167.

into mythic-symbolic language, one such linguistic region has been specified. Ideally, there are several similar regions dealing with biology, art, mathematics, music, politics, etc. The advantage of such a theory of language, in the context of this inquiry, is that it can account for mythic-symbolic language as a valid region or language in the context of other regions or languages. As such, the definition and interpretation of mythic-symbolic language as a valid form is secured.

6. Mythic-Symbolic Language and a Global Understanding of Man

By employing Husserlian epistemology we are free from the necessity of making the historical-evolutionary distinction between the logical and the prelogical that prejudiced the prior view. Consequently, it was no longer necessary to negate mythic-symbolic language in its primary form. Turning to language per se, it was possible to find a hermeneutic which began with a positive acknowledgement of the validity of mythic-symbolic language. We are now able to move to a structural interpretation. Thus far, we have shown how such a language can be affirmed because nothing has been said about the necessity of such language. To show that such language has a necessary as well as valid function, one must go beyond an analysis of the structure of mythic-symbolic language to its correlation with the understanding of man contained within that language.

The philosophy of Paul Ricoeur represents an attempt to consider freedom in relationship to its limitation in three ways defined in a context that moves from the abstract to the concrete. This interpretation can be sustained by the problem of the first Volume of *The Philosophy of The Will* wherein freedom is informed and limited by nature, the voluntary is informed and limited by the involuntary. In *Fallible Man* freedom is limited by the possibility of fault. In *The Symbolism of Evil* the actual confession of the experience of evil in the language of symbo land myth, the language of avowal, occurs. The drive toward the concrete represents the drive toward mythic-symbolic language. The proposition that exists as a result of the movement of Ricoeur's thought is: *mythic-symbolic language is necessary for a global understanding of man*. The argument is simply this. One must risk an encounter with the symbols and myths of evil if he is ever to understand fully the actual human experience of evil and the real limitation placed upon freedom. This kind of language functions for a philosophical anthropology in a distinctive way. First, mythic-symbolic language has a necessary function for the establishment of a global anthropology: second, mythic-symbolic language is constitutive for thought on freedom and evil.

The question that is the burden of this inquiry is, what distinguishes mythic-symbolic language from other forms of discourse? Our answer is that *mythic-symbolic discourse is constitutive for the human quest for freedom*. When men have sought to express their desire for freedom in contradistinction to the correlate experience of limitation, they have used mythic-symbolic language to do it. One may speculate to the extent to which man continues to desire freedom beyond the contingencies of ordinary experience, he will employ this kind of language to do it. To those who have attempted to dispense with mythic-symbolic language as irrelevant to contemporary men, we are in a position to point to the distinctive function of mythic-symbolic language as a refutation.

7. Conclusion

The beginning of this chapter as well as the beginning of this essay stated the problem of a negative correlation between mythic-symbolic language and philosophical anthropology. In previous chapters we sought to show that other alternatives were available by an analysis of alternative views of mythic-symbolic forms and the related notions about man. In this discussion, we sought to use those insights for a constructive correlation, placing those findings in a theoretical context. Consonant with that intention, it was necessary to refer to an anthropological judgment about consciousness, a theory of language inclusive of a hermeneutic and a definition, and finally, to return to the anthropological consequences of that theory to achieve our end. Now we have that end. We have attempted to show that a positive correlation between mythic-symbolic language and philosophical anthropology is possible not only in terms of other viewpoints but theoretically and constructively.

B. METHODOLOGY

1. Hermeneutic Phenomenology and the Philosophy of Religion

A schematic definition of the philosophy of religion is summed up in the phrase, "reflection on religion." If general agreement on this definition of philosophy of religion is possible, it is more difficult to define the context of the term religion. In Schleiermacher's *The Christian Faith* there is an argument which presents one type of solution to the problem.

The piety which forms the basis for all ecclesiastical communions is considered purely in itself, neither a Knowing, nor a Doing, but a modification of Feeling, of immediate self-consciousness.[9]

From this point of view, the content of religion is self-consciousness. If it were possible to rely solely upon the Husserlian "consciousness" model, it would seem that the definition of the philosophy of religion that would be a logical consequence of this study would be a restatement of the Schleiermacher position. However, on the basis of the proposed revision of the Husserlian argument, it is not consciousness, but consciousness as it is presented in the context of language that functions as *the pre-reflexive basis for philosophical reflection*. Consonant with that redefinition, we may define the philosophy of religion as that discipline which reflects upon mythic-symbolic language. Conversely, mythic-symbolic language functions as the foundation which makes reflection possible.

The first methodological step is directly in line with the previous discussion. It follows from Ricoeur's notion that thinking about a mythic-symbolic form begins with that form. The process of philosophical reflection then, begins on the basis of an encounter with mythic-symbolic language, or, to be specific, the reflective process begins on the basis of an encounter with the component parts of a mythic-symbolic language.

The basis for this first methodological step in the process of philosophical reflection upon the mythic-symbolic form has already been provided by the previous theoretical statement. It is possible to assume that the hermeneutical starting point, deemed so important for an adequate approach to mythic-symbolic forms, can be incorporated into this reflective analysis.

Equally important, is the matter of the definition of these component parts of a mythic-symbolic language. It would be possible to rely upon the definition of symbol and myth given by Ricoeur, a definition stated in theoretical context in this chapter. If the philosophy of religion can be defined as reflection upon mythic-symbolic language, the associated assumption is that such language can be defined as valid because it contains a claim to uniqueness, a claim to represent a dimension of

[9] Friedrich Schleiermacher, *The Christian Faith* (Edinburgh: T. and T. Clark, 1928), p. 5

experience, and a claim to be constitutive for a type of meaning. As a consequence, the procedure of the philosophy of religion is influenced by this methodology because the reflective process begins from the symbol and myth. Therefore, the purpose of reflection is not to reduce mythic-symbolic forms to a secondary, but supposedly, more adequate language. Reflection begins with the symbol and myth and it proceeds from them.

The second methodological step involves the particular investment of the philosopher of religion in reflection upon the nature of man. This is the problem of the ground and direction of the reflective process. It has been argued throughout this essay that the manner in which a mythic-symbolic form may be specified is by reference to its anthropological focus. Methodologically this means that the philosophy of religion is correlative with philosophical anthropology. There are several reasons for suggesting this as a possibility based on the conclusions of the prior discussion. First, mythic-symbolic forms are constitutive for the human quest for totality; second, mythic-symbolic forms are constitutive for the human desire for freedom; third, mythic-symbolic language is constitutive for man's experience of and attempt to overcome limitation. The investigation of mythic-symbolic language has significance in terms of its contribution to our understanding of man. It is the responsibility of the philosophy of religion to specify the significance of the mythic-symbolic form for the precise purpose of placing it in the context of philosophical anthropology.

These two methodological steps enable us to specify what generally may be called the contribution of hermeneutic phenomenology to the philosophy of religion. Philosophic reflection on symbolic and mythic forms introduces a principle of rationality into the process of analysis. The introduction of this principle involves both a risk and a possibility in the sense that the risk involved in reflection on symbol and myth is reductionism, while rationality reduces the plurality of meaning present in a mythic-symbolic form by making it into a single meaning. The possibility that is presented by reflection upon symbolic and mythic forms is that the philosophic understanding is enriched by the process. In Ricoeur's terms, this kind of process is necessary for a global understanding of man. The problem becomes one of discovering how it is possible to reflect upon symbolic and mythic forms without diminishing their richness, that is, without returning to the dilemma of reductionism. Ricoeur's discussion of the symbolism of evil illustrates well the problem of philosophic reflection on symbolic forms as it affects the philosophy of religion. As we have seen the two types of reduction seen to be characteristic of western reflection on the problem of evil are the gnostic and the allegorical modes of reflection.[10] Each in its own way distorts the richness and multivalence of the symbolic-mythic form. In terms of the two structural components of the symbolism of evil, the priority of evil and evil as one's responsible creation, allegorization has meant the separation of the symbolic intention of the symbolism of evil from its literal intention. This reduces the problems of evil to an element of negation. For Ricoeur, Hegel is the prime example of that alternative because in his thought, evil becomes an element of negation between being and becoming.[11] In contrast to the allegorical position, the gnostic alternative has attempted to build systems of explanation for the fact that man is implicated already in the process of evil. Ricoeur's example is Augustine's battle against the Pelagians and his use and development of the doctrine of original sin to explain the priority of evil.[12]

Philosophic reflection on primary symbols has resulted in attempts to lift out one of the structural components of a particular symbolism and center upon it at the expense of others. This is the tendency to rational reflection on symbolic forms. But how can philosophical reflection proceed from the data provided by a mythic-symbolic language? We arrive here at the third methodological step for a philosophy of religion. It is our belief that a philosophical analysis informed by the findings of the history of religions can proceed on the basis of structural or morphological analysis as well as the discoveries provided by the philosopher himself. Most important, however, is the fact that the first level of analysis is a comparison of mythic-symbolic forms. One begins to understand the meaning of particular mythic-symbolic forms by a process of structural association and integration.

Ricoeur's approach to the symbolism of evil exemplifies the kind of structural analysis the philosophy of religion could incorporate. We do not wish to suggest that the philosophy of religion can take over the task of the historian of religion. The philosopher of religion can follow the procedure outlined by the history of religions which provides data for philosophical reflection. By incorporating the structural and comparative approach into the methodology of the philosophy of re-

---

[10] Paul Ricoeur, "The Hermeneutics of Symbols and Philosophical Reflection," *International Philosophical Quarterly*, II, No. 2 (1963), 204.

[11] *Ibid.*, 217.

[12] *Ibid.*, 210.

ligion, we simply are suggesting the logical procedure that would be followed.

The value of the philosophic quest for total rational explanation of symbolic structures and forms is undeniable. It represents the philosopher's nostalgia for complete clarity. The principle of clarity and rationality, however, can also reach its limitation. Reflection upon the symbolism of evil may reduce the problem of evil to a simple matter of human responsibility. Such an explanation fails to deal with the element of the tragic, the implication of the self in the very process of evil. Since there is no way to explain evil rationally, it is precisely at this juncture that thought reaches its limit.

Ricoeur has suggested that the method which can be followed in reflection upon the symbol comes under the rubric, "the symbol invites thought." In other words, it is in the language of symbols and myths, the language of avowal, that one finds an original human expression of the experience of evil. This expression of the experience of evil can inform reflection as a pre-reflexive base; it marks a starting point for philosophical reflection. On the other hand, reflection reaches its limit in the experience of tragedy.

It seems necessary then to suggest that reflection upon the symbol is a circular process. If we are to follow the methodological process suggested by the phrase "the symbol invites thought," its conclusion should read, "thought invites the symbol." The latter phrase implies the following: When thought about the symbol reaches its limit in rational reflection, it is driven back to the symbol or symbolism with which it is associated. For documentation, it is possible to turn to the symbolism of evil. When reflection reaches its limit in the tragic, it is driven back to the symbolism of evil. Evil is simply there. It is present and symbolized as stain. But when reflection is driven back, one recognizes that the symbolism of evil is itself incomplete. At this point the symbolism of evil is complemented by the symbolism of liberation. The possibility that is revealed when reflection reaches its limit, is therefore, to return to the symbol. In this instance, the return to the symbol is informed by the direction in which the symbol itself points. The method of reflection that may be incorporated in this third methodological step for the philosophy of religion may lead us to conclude that *the symbol invites thought, while thought invites the symbol.* At this point, philosophic reflection continues in a mode of comparison while introducing a motif of reflection. This third level of reflection constitutes a hermeneutic circle extending from a direct encounter with the symbol to an understanding of its meaning inclusive of reflection.

On the basis of the prior theoretical foundation, a threefold methodology for the philosophy of religion may be advanced. First, philosophical reflection can begin with the component parts of a mythic-symbolic language as its pre-reflexive base. Second, the direction of the philosophy of religion can be defined as its specification of the mythic-symbolic form in the context of a philosophical anthropology. Third, the philosophy of religion can follow the hermeneutic procedure implicit in the phrase, "the symbol invites thought ,while thought invites the symbol," incorporating comparative, structural, and reflective motifs.

WHAT IS A TEXT?
EXPLANATION AND INTERPRETATION

PAUL RICOEUR

This essay will be devoted principally to the debate between two basic attitudes which one can adopt in regard to a text. These two attitudes were summed up, in the time of Wilhelm Dilthey, by the two words "explain" and "interpret." Dilthey called *explanation* that model of intelligibility borrowed from the natural sciences and extended to the historical sciences by the positivistic schools, and he took *interpretation* as a derived form of *understanding* in which he saw the basic approach of the "human sciences" (*Geisteswissenschaften*), the only one which can do justice to the basic difference between these sciences and the "natural sciences." I would like here to examine the outcome of this opposition in the light of the conflicts between contemporary schools. The notion of explanation has, indeed, shifted positions; it no longer stems from the natural sciences but from strictly linguistic models. As for the notion of interpretation, it has, in modern hermeneutics, undergone deep transformations which set it off from the psychological notion of understanding, in Dilthey's sense of the term. It is this new situation of the problem perhaps less contradictory and more fruitful, which I would like to explore. But before entering into the new concepts of explanation and interpretation, I would like to devote some time to a preliminary question which in fact will determine all the rest of our investigation. The question is this: What is a text?

I. WHAT IS A TEXT?

Let us call a text every utterance or set of utterances fixed by writing. According to this definition, the fixation by writing is constitutive of the text itself. But what is fixed by writing? We have said: every utterance or group of utterances. Is this to say that these utterances must have been previously enunciated physically or mentally, that all writing has been, at least in a potential way, first of all speech? In short, how does it stand with the relation of the text to speech?

The psychological and sociological priority of speech over writing is not in question. *Psychological priority*: if by speech we mean the production of a particular discourse by a particular speaker addressing himself to a hearer who may or may not understand what the first speaker means, this kind of human experience precedes that of writing. *Sociological priority*: the need for a preservation of spoken language by the means of some kind of fixation, inscription or recording may be assigned to a rather late stage of economical and political development. One can however wonder if the late appearance of writing has not provoked a radical change in our relation to the very utterance of our discourse. That which is fixed by writing is a discourse which certainly one could have spoken but *which one writes precisely* because one does not speak. The fixation by means of writing occurs in the plan of speech itself, that is, in the plan where speech could have arisen. One can then wonder whether a text is not truly a text when it is not just limited to recording a prior speech, but when it invites directly in written words the meaning of the utterance.

That which could give insight to this idea of a direct relation between writing and the meaning intended by the utterance is the function which reading plays in regard to that which is written. Indeed, a written text calls for a reading which later will allow us to introduce both concepts of explanation and interpretation as specific kinds of reading. For the time being, let us say that the reader takes the place of the listener, just as writing takes the place of speaking. Indeed, the writing – reading relation is not just a particular instance of the speaking – answering relation. It is not an instance of dialogue. Whereas dialogue is an exchange of questions and answers, there is no exchange of this sort between the writer and his reader; the writer does not answer the reader. Rather, the book introduces a shift between the act of writing and the act of reading, between which two acts there is no communication: the reader is absent from the writing of the book, the writer is absent from its reading. In this way the text produces a double effacement (occultation) of reader and writer; it is in this way it gets substituted for the relation by means of dialogue which immediately binds together the voice of the one and the ear of the other.

This substitution of reading in the precise place of a dialogue which does not occur is so evident that when we have the occasion of meeting an author and of speaking with him (about his book, for instance), we experience a kind of disturbance in that very special relation which we have with the author in and through his work. I like to say sometimes that to read a book is to consider its author as already dead and the book as posthumous. Indeed, it is when the author is dead that the relation to his book becomes complete and, in a way, intact. The author can no longer respond; it only remains to read his work.

This difference between the act of reading and the act of dialogue confirms our hypothesis that writing is a process similar to speech, parallel to speech, an operation which takes its place and in a way intercepts it. This is why we were able to say that writing is a direct inscription of this intention, even if, historically and psychologically, writing began as a graphic transcription of speech signs. This liberation of writing whereby it gets substituted for speech is the birth of a text.

At present, what happens now to the utterance itself when it is directly inscribed instead of being pronounced? Emphasis has always been placed on the most striking characteristic of writing, that it preserves discourse and makes of it an archives available for individual and collective memory. Added to this is the fact that the linearization of symbols allows for an analytic and distinctive translation of all the successive and discrete traits of language and thus increases its efficiency. Is this all that it does? Preservation and efficiency still only characterize the transcription of oral language into graphic signs. The liberation of a text from vocal existence results in a veritable upheaval as much in the relations between language and the world as in the relation between language and the different subjectivities involved, that of the author and that of the reader.

Let us call reference or referential relation the relation between language and the reality (whatever it may be) *about* which something is said in a sequence of discourse; to speak is to say something *about* something *to* somebody; let us put aside for a moment this relation of discourse to somebody else, in order to focus on the relation "about" something; this 'about" designates the referent of the discourse. This referential relation is, as one knows, borne by the sentence, which is the first and simplest unity of discourse. This referential function is so important that it compensates, so to say, for another characteristic of language which is the separation of signs from things: by means of the referential function language "returns' so to say, to reality, which it tries to grasp, to represent, to express. What we call the symbolic function of language is a kind of balance between a process of *difference* which separates the world of signs from the world of things and a process of *reference*, which "pours back" language into the universe. It is this subtle balance between *difference* and *reference* which speech preserves and which writing destroys.

In speech the function of reference is linked to the role of the *situation of discourse* within the exchange of language itself: in exchanging speech, the speakers are present to each other, but also to the circumstantial setting of discourse, not only the perceptual surroundings, but also the cultural background known by both speakers. It is in relation to this situation that discourse is fully meaningful; the reference to reality is in the last analysis reference to that reality which can be pointed out "around" the speakers, "around," so to speak, the instance of discourse itself. Language is, moreover, well equipped to insure this anchorage; the demonstrative articles, the spatial and temporal adverbs, the personal pronouns, the tenses of the verb, and in general all the ostensive indicators of language serve to anchor discourse in the circumstantial reality which surrounds the instance of discourse. Thus, in living speech, the *ideal* meaning of what one says bends towards a *real* reference, namely to that "about which" one speaks; at its limit this real reference tends to get confused with an ostensive designation wherein speech joins up with the indicative gesture, that of pointing out.

This is no longer the case when a text takes the place of speech. The shifting of references towards ostensive designation (showing) is intercepted, at the same time that dialogue is interrupted by the text. I say indeed intercepted and not suppressed; it is here that I will shortly take up my distance from what I shall call the ideology of the absolute text which is based on an undue hypostasis of the rightful remarks we have just made. A text, we shall see, is not without reference; it will be precisely the task of reading, as interpretation, to actualize the reference. At least, in this suspension wherein reference is deferred, in the sense that it is postponed, a text is somehow "in the air," outside of the world or without a world; by means of this obliteration of all relation to the world, every text is free to enter into relation with all the other texts which come to take the place of the circumstantial reality shown by living speech.

This relation of one text to another, in the disappearance of the world about which one speaks, engenders the quasi-world of texts or *literature*. Such is the upheaval which affects discourse itself, when the movement of reference towards designation (showing) is intercepted by a text, words cease to efface themselves in front of things; written words become words for their own sake.

II. STRUCTURAL ANALYSIS AS "EXPLANATION"

We are now prepared to introduce the opposition between explanation and interpretation as a consequence of the autonomous status of the written text as regards speech. What we called masking (occultation) of the surrounding world by the quasi-world of texts gives rise to two possibilities. As readers, we can remain in the suspense of the text and treat it as a worldless and authorless text, in which case we explain it by means of its internal relations, its structure. Or else we can remove the text's suspense, accomplish it in a way similar to speech, returning it to living communication, in which case we interpret it. These two possibilities both belong to the act of reading, and reading consists in a dialectical interplay of these two attitudes.

Let us take them up separately, before considering their connections. We can make the text into a first kind of reading, a reading which acknowledges, so to speak, the text's interception of all the relations with a world which can be shown and with subjectivities who can converse. This transfer into the "place" where the text stands constitutes a special project in regard to the text, that of prolonging its suspension of the referential relation to the world and the reference to the author as the speaking subject. By means of this special project, the reader decides to stay within the "place of the text" and within the "enclosure" of this place. On the basis of this choice, the text has no outside; it has but an inside; it aims at no transcendence, as would speech which is directed *to* someone, *about* something.

This project is not only possible but legitimate. Indeed, the constitution of the text as text and the system of text as literature justifies the interception of this double transcendence of speech towards a world and another person. On this basis an explanatory attitude in regard to the text becomes possible.

Now, unlike what Dilthey thought, this explanatory attitude is in no way borrowed from an area of knowledge and an epistemological model other than that of language itself. It does not rely on a naturalistic model extended only secondarily to the human sciences. The natural-mind opposition is not even operative here. If something is borrowed, it takes place inside the same field, that of semiology or semiotics. It is indeed possible to treat texts according to the explanatory rules which linguistics successfully applied to elementary systems of signs which constitute language (langue) in opposition to speech. As is known, the language – speech distinction is the basic distinction which furnishes linguistics with a homogeneous object; whereas speech belongs to physiology, psychology, sociology, language, as the system of rules of which speech is the exception, belongs only to linguistics. As is also known, linguistics considers only systems of entities which possess no absolute meaning and which are defined only by their difference from all the other unities. These unities, which are either merely distinctive like those of phonological articulation or significant like those of lexical articulation, are oppositive entities or unities. It is the interplay of oppositions and their combinations on the basis of an inventory of discreet unities which defines the notion of structure in linguistics. It is this structural model which furnishes the type of explanatory behavior which we are now going to see applied to a text, mainly by French structuralists.

Even before beginning this undertaking, it might be objected that laws which are valid only for language as distinct from speech could not be applied to a text. Is not a text, one might say, while not being speech still in the same position as speech in regard to language (langue)? Is it not necessary to oppose in an overall way speech as a succession of utterances, that is, in the last analysis, as a succession of sentences, to language? Is not the speech – writing distinction secondary in regard to this language – discourse distinction, language and speech occupying the same position as discourse? These remarks are perfectly legitimate and permit us to think that that explanatory model characterized as structural does not exhaust the field of possible attitudes in regard to a text. But even before saying what the limit of this explanatory attitude is, it is necessary to grasp its fruitfulness. The working hypothesis of all structural analysis of texts is this: in spite of the fact that writing occupies the same position as speech in regard to language, namely that of discourse, the specificity of writing in regard to actual speech is based on structural characteristics which may be treated as analogies of language within discourse. The working hypothesis is perfectly legitimate; it consists in saying that under certain conditions the larger unities of language, that is to say, the unities of higher order than the sentence, are organized in a way similar to that of the small unities of language, that is, the unities of an order lower than the sentence, those precisely which belong to the domain of linguistics.

In his *Anthropologie structurale*,[1] Claude Levi-Straus formulates in the following way this working hypothesis in regard to one category of texts, that of myths: "Like every linguistic entity, the myth is made up of constitutive unities; these constitutive unities imply the presence of those which generally occur in the structure of language, namely phonemes, morphemes, semantemes. Each form differs from the one which precedes it by a higher degree of complexity. For this reason we will call the elements which properly belong to the myth (and which are the most complex of all): large constitutive unities." By means of this working hypothesis, the large unities which are at least the same size as the sentence and which, put together, form the narrative proper to the myth will be able to be treated according to the same rules as the smallest unities known to linguistics. It is in order to insist on this likeness that Claude Levi-Strauss speaks of mythemes, just as one speaks of phonemes, morphemes, etc. But in order to remain within the limits of the analogy between mythemes and the lower level linguistic unities, the analysis of texts will have to operate on the same sort of abstraction as that practiced by the phonologist. For the latter, the phoneme is not a concrete sound, in an absolute sense, with its acoustic quality; (it is a function defined by commutation which resolves itself into its oppositive value in relation to all the others). In this sense, it is not, to speak like Saussure, a "substance" but a form, that is to say, an interplay of relations. Similarly, a mytheme is not one of the sentences of a myth but an oppositive value attached to several individual sentences forming, in the terminology of Levi-Strauss, a "bundle of relations": "It is only in the form of a combination of such bundles that the constitutive unities acquire a meaning-function."[2] What is here called meaning-function is not at all what the myth means, its philosophical or existential content or intention, but the arrangement, the disposition of mythemes, in short, the structure of the myth.

I would like to recall here briefly the analysis which, according to this method, Levi-Strauss offers of the Oepidus myth. He separates into four columns the sentences of the myth. In the first column he places all those which speak of an over-esteemed parental relationship (for example, Oedipus weds Jocasta, his mother, Antigone buries Polynices, her brother, in spite of the order not to); in the second column are to be found the same relations but affected with the opposite

---

[1] Claude Levi-Strauss, *Anthropologie structurale*. Paris: Librairie Plon, 1958, p. 233.
[2] *Ibid.*, p. 234.

sign, and under-esteemed or devaluated parental relationship (Oedipus kills his father, Laios, Eteocles kills his brother Polynices); the third column is concerned with monsters and their destruction; the fourth groups together all the proper names whose meanings suggest a difficulty to walk straight (lame, clumsy, swollen foot). A comparison of the four columns brings out a correlation. Between one and two what we have are parental relationships by turns overesteemed or underesteemed; between three and four we have an affirmation and then a negation of man's autochthony (aboriginal, indigenous): "It would thereby result that the fourth column holds the same relation with column three as column one does with column two...; the overestimation of the blood relationship is, in regard to its underestimation, like the attempt to escape from the autochthonous situation and the impossibility of therein succeeding." The myth thus appears as a sort of logical instrument which draws together contradictions in order to overcome them: "the impossibility of connecting groups of relations is thus overcome (or, more exactly, replaced) by the affirmation that the two contradictory relations are identical between themselves to the degree that each, like the other, is self-contradictory."[3] We will return shortly to the conclusion of the formal analysis; let us limit ourselves (now) to stating it.

We can indeed say that we have explained the myth, but not that we have interpreted it. We have, by means of structural analysis, brought out the logic of the operations which relate the four bundles of relations among themselves; this logic constitutes "the structural law of the myth under consideration."[4] It will not fail to be noticed that this law is pre-eminently an object of reading and not at all of speaking, in the sense of a reciting where the power of the myth would be actuated in a particular situation. Here the text is but a text; and reading inhabits it only as a text, thanks to the suspension of its meaning for us, to the postponement of all actualization by present speech.

I have just taken an example from the field of myths; I could take another from a neighboring field, that of folklore narratives. This field has been explored by the Russian formalists of the school of Propp and by the French specialists of the structural analysis of narratives, Roland Barthes and Greimas. The same postulates as those of Levi-Strauss are to be found in these authors as well: the unities above the sentence have the same composition as the unities below the sentence; the mean-

---

[3] Levi-Strauss, *Anthropologie structurale*, p. 239.
[4] *Ibid.*, p. 241.

ing of an element is its ability to enter into relation with other elements and with all of the work. These postulates together define the enclosure of the narrative; the task of structural analysis will then consist in operating a segmentation (the horizontal aspect) and then establishing various levels of integration of the parts in the whole (the hierarchical aspect). But the unities of action, which are segmented and organized in that way have nothing to do with psychological traits susceptible of being lived or with behavioral segments susceptible of falling under a behaviorist psychology; the extremities of these sequences are only switching points in the narrative, such that if one element is changed, all the rest are different. One recognizes here a transposition of the commutative method from the phonological level to the level of narrative unities. The logic of action consists then in a linking together of action kernels (noyaux d'action) which all together constitute the narrative's structural continuity; the application of this technic results in a "dechronologizing" of the narrative, so as to make apparent the narrative logic underlying narrative time. Ultimately, the narrative is reduced to a combination (combinatoire) of a few dramatic unities: promising, betraying, hindering, aiding, etc., which would thus be the paradigms of action. A sequence is thus a succession of action kernels, each one closing off an alternative opened up by the preceding one. These elementary unities fit in with larger unities; for example, the encounter embraces elementary actions such as approaching, summoning, greeting, etc. To explain a narrative is to get hold of this symphonic structure of segmental actions.

To this chain of actions correspond relations of the same sort between the "acting character" of the narrative. By this we do not at all mean psychological subjects, but formalized roles correlative to formalized actions. The acting characters are defined only by the predicates of action, by the semantic axis of the sentence and narrative: the one who does the act, the one to whom, with whom, etc. the action is done; it is the one who promises, who receives the promise, the giver, the receiver, etc. Structural analysis thus brings out a hierarchy of acting characters correlative to the hierarchy of *actions*.

It remains then to assemble the narrative as a whole and to put it back into narrative communication. It is then a discourse addressed by the narrator to a receiver. But, for structural analysis, the two interlocutors must be looked for in the text and nowhere else; the narrator is designated only by the narrative signs which themselves belong to the very constitution of the narrative. There is no longer anything beyond these three levels (level of actions, level of acting characters, level of narration) which belongs to the semiologist's science; there is but the world of the users of the narrative which itself eventually falls under other semiological disciplines (social, economic, ideological systems), but which are no longer ones of a linguistic sort. This transposition of a linguistic model to the theory of the narrative perfectly verifies our initial remark: explanation today is no longer a concept borrowed from the natural sciences and transferred into a different field, that of written monuments; it procedes from the same sphere of language, thanks to an analogical transfer of the small unities of language (phonemes and lexemes) to the large unities subsequent to the sentence, such as narrative, folklore, myth. As a result, interpretation will no longer be confronted with a model foreign to the human sciences, a model of intelligibility, borrowed from a science, linguistics, belonging to the same field of human sciences. As a result, it will be on the same ground, inside of the same sphere of language that explanation and interpretation will dispute each other.

III. TOWARDS A NEW CONCEPT OF INTERPRETATION

Let us now consider the other attitude which one can adopt in regard to a text, that one which we have called interpretation. It is first of all by opposing it to the preceding one, in a way similar to that of Dilthey, that we can introduce it. But it will be possible to gradually reach a relation more closely complementary and reciprocal between explanation and interpretation.

Let us start off once again from the act of reading. Two ways of reading, we have said, are offered to us. By reading we can prolong and reinforce the suspension affecting the text's reference to the environment of a world and the audience of speaking subjects; this is the explanatory attitude. But we can also bring an end to this suspension and complete the text in actual discourse. It is this second attitude which is the genuine aim of reading. The other sort of reading would not even be possible if it were not first of all apparent that the text, as writing, waits and calls for a reading; if a reading is possible, it is indeed because the text is not closed in on itself but open out onto something else. By any supposition reading is a linking together of a new discourse to the discourse of the text. The linking reveals, in the very constitution of the text, an original capacity of being reenacted, which is its *open* character. Interpretation is the concrete result of this openness and of this linking together. How?

Our first concept of interpretation will still be close to that of Dilthey. We may characterize it, in general terms, as *appropriation*. Truth to tell, this meaning will not be abandoned, it will only be mediated by explanation itself, instead of being opposed to it in an immediate and rather naive way.

By appropriation I mean several things. I mean first that the interpretation of a text ends up in the self-interpretation of a subject who henceforth understands himself better. This completion of text understanding in self-understanding characterizes the sort of reflective philosophy which I call concrete reflection. Hermeneutics and reflective philosophy are here correlative and reciprocal: on the one hand, self-understanding provided a round-about way of understanding of the cultural signs in which the self contemplates himself and forms himself; on the other hand, the understanding of a text is not an end in itself and for itself; it mediates the relation to himself of a subject who, in the short circuit of immediate reflection, would not find the meaning of his own life. Thus it is necessary to say just as strongly that reflection is nothing without mediation by means of signs and cultural works and that explanation is nothing if it is not incorporated, as an intermediary stage, in the process of self-understanding. In short, in hermeneutical reflection – or in reflective hermeneutics – the constitution of *self* and that of meaning are contemporaneous.

The term appropriation entails two further characteristics. One of the aims of all hermeneutics is to fight against cultural distance; by cultural distance I mean not only the temporal distance but the kind of estrangement in regard to the system of values to which the cultural background of the text belongs. In this sense, interpretation "brings together," "equalizes," – all of which is to genuinely render *proper* (one's own) that which was previously foreign.

But, above all, the characterization of interpretation as appropriation is meant to draw attention to the kind of *actuality* which belongs to the process of interpretation. Reading is like the performance of a musical score: it betokens the fulfillment, the actualization of the semantic virtualities of the text. This third trait is the most important; for it is the interpretations with self-interpretation, the overcoming of cultural distance; this character of actualization reveals the decisive function of reading, namely that it achieves the discourse of the text in a dimension similar to speech. Speech too is an event; speech is discourse as event; speech is the instance of discourse, as Benvenito says; in speech and by speech, the sentences which constitute the discourse as discourse signify *hic et nunc*. Reading – as the actualization of the text – gives to writing a similar achievement: the actualized text finds at last an environment and an audience, a world and an intersubjective dimension. In interpretation, we shall say, reading becomes like speech. I do not say, becomes speech, for reading never equals an exchange of speech, a dialogue. But reading is concretely accomplished in an act which is, in regard to the text, what speech is in regard to language, namely, an event and instance of discourse. In explanation the text had only internal relations, a structure; in interpretation it has now a significance, that is, an accomplishment in the subject's own discourse. By means of its structure the text had only a semiological dimension; by means of the actualization, it now has a semantic dimension.

Let us pause here. Our discussion has reached a critical point: interpretation, understood as appropriation, still remains exterior to explanation in the sense of structural analysis. We keep opposing them as two attitudes between which it would be necessary to choose.

I would like now to overcome this non-dialectical opposition and make apparent the inner connections which render structural analysis and hermeneutics complementary. For this it is necessary to show how each of the two attitudes which we have opposed refers back to the other by means of characteristics which are proper to it.

Let us return to the examples of structural analysis which are borrowed from the theory of myth and narrative. We tried to hold ourselves to a notion of sense (or meaning) which would be strictly reducible to the arrangement of the elements within the text. As a matter of fact no one remains with a conception as formal as this of the sense (or meaning) of a narrative or myth. For instance, what Levi-Strauss calls a "mytheme," and which is in his opinion the constitutive unity of the myth, is expressed in a sentence which has a meaning, in the sense of a referential intention of its own: Oepidus kills his father, weds his mother, etc. Is one to say that the structural explanation neutralizes the meaning proper to these and those sentences as merely to retain their positions in the myth? But the bundle of relations to which Levi-Strauss reduces the mythemes is still of the same order as the sentence, and the interplay of oppositions which is instigated at this very abstract level is still of the same order as the sentence. If one speaks of "overevaluated" or "under-evaluated blood relationships," of man's "autochthony" or "non-autochthony," these relations can still be written in the form of a structure: the blood is not as high as the social relationship, for instance the prohibition of incest, etc. In short, the contradiction which according to Levi-Strauss the myth attempts to resolve, expresses itself in meaningul relationships. Levi-Strauss admits it, in spite of himself, where he writes: "the reason for these choices becomes apparent if it is recognized that mythical thought proceeds from the becoming aware (de la pride de conscience) of certain opposition and tends towards their progressive mediation."[5] And again: "the myth is a sort of logical root destined to achieve a mediation between life and death."[6] In the background of the myth there is a question which is a highly meaningful one, a question about life and death: "Is one born from one or from two"? This question expresses anxiety and agony concerning the origin: whence does man come? Is he born of the earth, is he born of his parents? There would be no contradiction, and no attempts to resolve the contradiction, if there were not meaningful questions, meaningful conjectures concerning the origin and the end of man. Is it possible to put within brackets this function of the myth as a narrative of the origins? I do not think so. In fact, structural analysis does not succeed including this function: it merely postpones it. If the myth is a logical operation, it does not play this role between any proposition whatsoever, but between utterances which point towards border-line situations: birth and death, sexuality and suffering, origin and end. Structural analysis, far from getting rid of this radical questioning, restores it at a level of even higher rationality. Would it not then be the function of structural analysis to put into question a superficial semantics, that of the apparent narrative, so as to make manifest a depth-semantics, which is the latent narrative, or, if I may say so, the live semantics of the myth? I readily believe that if such were not the living function of structural analysis, it would be reduced to a sterile game of combinations; the myth would be robbed even of the function which Levi-Strauss himself recognizes it to have where he says that mythical thought proceeds from the awareness of certain oppositives and tends towards their progressive mediation. This awareness is that of the enigmas of existence and end which mythic thought generates. To eliminate this meaningful intention would be to reduce the theory of myth to a necrology of the meaningless discourses of mankind. If, on the contrary, one considers structural analysis as a stage – and a necessary one –

[5] Levi-Strauss, *Anthropologie structurale*, p. 248.
[6] *Ibid.*, p. 243.

between a naive interpretation and a critical interpretation, between a superficial interpretation and a depth interpretation, then it would seem possible to locate explanation and interpretation at two different stages of a hermeneutical arch and to integrate the opposed attitudes of explanation and understanding within the unique concrete act of reading.

We will take a step further in the direction of this reconciliation between explanation and interpretation by submitting to a parallel critique our initial concept of interpretation. To interpret, we said, is to appropriate *hic et nunc* for ourselves the intention of the text. In saying that, we remained within the enclosure of Dilthey's "understanding." Now, what we have just said concerning the depth-semantics of the text to which structural analysis refers is an invitation for us to understand that the intended meaning is not the supposed intention of the author, the vivid experience of *the writer*, into which we should have to transport ourselves, but rather that which *the text* wants to say. Not the psychological intention of the author, but the *injunction* of the text. What the text wants, is to orient our thought according to it. The sense of the text is the direction which it opens up for our thought.

This concept of sense as direction for thought leads us to a new definition of interpretation which would be less a subjective operation than an objective process; less an act *on* the text, than an act *of* the text. This process of interpretation has something to do with the depth semantics of the text delivered by structural analysis; it is this depth semantics which is to understand in dynamic terms; whereas the structure constitutes the statics of the text, the depth semantics is itself a process of meaning; it requires a fresh interpretation because it is itself an interpretation, this interpretation which I called the act of the text.

I will take an example in the field of biblical exegesis. Werner H. Schmidt has shown the account of creation according to Genesis 1–2, relies on the interplay of two narratives, a *Totbericht*, in which creation is expressed merely in terms of action: "God made...," and a *Wortbericht*, in which creation proceeds from the word: "God said, and there was..." The first narrative plays the role of tradition and the second that of interpretation. Within the same text, therefore, tradition and interpretation constitute the two poles of the meaning as process. To interpret the text is follow the pattern of thought opened by this process. In that way, interpretation is the act of the text, before being an act of exegesis; it is like an arrow borne by the text itself, indicating the direction for the exegetical work.

This concept of objective interpretation, or, if we may say, of intra-textual interpretation has nothing unusual about it – it even has roots in an older tradition than the concept of subjective interpretation which is definitely modern. Aristotle called hermeneia (interpretation) the very act of language on things; unlike the hermeneutical technique of the augurs and interpreters of oracles, which announces the herme-neutic of romanticism, *hermeneia* designates the process of language; for Aristotle, to interpret is not what one does in a second language as applied to a first language; it is already what the first language does in mediating by signs our relation to things. Interpretation is thus, ac-cording to the commentary of Boethius on Aristotle's *Peri Hermeneias*, the very work of the *vox significativa per se ipsam aliquid significans, sive complexa, sive incomplexa.*

Indeed, interpretation in Aristotle's sense does not cover over con-cepts of interpretation which imply some kind of dynamic relation be-tween several layers of meaning within the same text (tradition and interpretation in the sense of Werner H. Schmidt); for Aristotle, inter-pretation means the semantic dimension of the noun, of the verb, of the sentence, in a word, of the discourse as such. Nevertheless, we may retain from Aristotle the idea that interpretation is interpretation *by* language before being interpretation *on* language.

The closest author which we may invoke for founding our concept of "objective" interpretation is Charles Saunders Peirce. According to Peirce, the relation of a "sign" to an "object" is such that another re-lation, that of a series of interpretants to the "signs" can graft itself onto the first. What is important for us here is that the relation of sign to interpretant is an open relation, in the sense that there is always another interpretant capable of mediating the first relation. This trian-gular relation between object, sign and interpretant, with the character of openness of the series of interpretants provides us with the best model for rebuilding our initial concept of interpretation. Indeed, it is with a great deal of caution that one should apply Peirce's concepts of interpretant to the interpretation of texts. This interpretant is an interpretant of signs, whereas our interpretation is an interpretation of utterances, of sentences, of discourse. Nevertheless this extension of Peirce's interpretant to texts is neither more nor less analogical than the transfer, with the structuralists, of the organized laws of unities from a level inferior to the sentence to unities of an equal or superior order than the sentence. In the case of structuralism, it is the phonological structure of language which serves as model for coding the structures of higher level. In our case, it is a characteristic of lexical unities – the triangular relation between object, sign and interpretant – which is carried over to the order of utterance and texts. If, therefore, one is perfectly aware of the analogical character of the transposition, it can be said: the open series of interpretants which grafts itself onto the relation of a sign to an object brings to light a triangualr relation, object-sign-interpretant, which can serve as a model for another triangle at the level of the text. In that new triangle, the object is the intended meaning of the text, the sign is the depth-semantics, unearthed by structural analysis, and the series of interpretants is the chain of interpretation produced by the interpretative community and incorporated into the dynamics of the text. In this chain the first interpretants serve as a tradition for the last interpretants which constitute the interpretation in the true sense of the term.

Enlightened in this way by the Aristotelian insight of interpretation and above all, by Peirce's concept of interpretant, we are in a position to "depsychologize" as much as possible our action of interpretation and to tie it up with the process which is at work in the text. As a result, for the exegete to interpret is to place himself in the direction initiated by this interpretative relation included in the text. The idea of interpretation, understood as appropriation, is not for all that eliminated; it is only postponed until the end of the process. It is the other end of what we have called the *hermeneutical arch*: it is the last pillar of the bridge, the anchor of the arch in the soil of lived experience. But the entire theory of hermeneutics consists in mediating the interpretation as appropriation by the series of interpretants which belong to the work of the text on itself. The appropriation poses then its arbitrariness to the degree that it is the recovery of what is at work, in labor, in the text. What the reader says is a re-saying which reenacts what the text says by itself.

At the end of this investigation it appears that reading is that concrete act in which the destiny of the text is accomplished. It is at the very heart of reading that explanation and interpretation are independently opposed and reconciled.

BIBLIOGRAPHY

PRIMARY SOURCES

Bultmann, Rudolf. *Essays, Philosophical and Theological*. London: SCM Press Ltd., 1955.
— *Existence and Faith*. New York: Living Age Books, 1960.
— *Jesus and the Word*. New York: Charles Scribner's Sons, 1958.
— *Jesus Christ and Mythology*. New York: Charles Scribner's Sons, 1958.
— *Kerygma and Myth*. New York: Harper and Brothers, 1957.
— *The Presence of Eternity*. New York: Harper and Brothers, 1957.
— *Theology of the New Testament*. 2 vols. New York: Charles Scribner's Sons, 1951–55.
— "The Christian Hope and the Problem of Demythologizing," *The Expository Times*, LXV, No. 8 (May, 1958), 228–30.
— "Demythologizing the Bible," *Current Religious Thought*, II, No. 1 (First Quarter, 1958), 7–9.
— "The Idea of God and Modern Man." In *Translating Theology into the Modern Age*. Edited by Robert W. Funk in association with Gerhard Ebeling. New York: Harper and Row, 1965. pp. 81–95.
Ricoeur, Paul. *De l'interprétation. Essai sur Freud*. Paris: Editions du Seuil, 1965.
— *Fallible Man*. Translated by Charles Kelbley. Chicago: Henry Regnery Co., 1965.
— *Freedom and Nature: The Voluntary and the Involuntary*. Translated by Erazim V. Kohak. Evanston: Northwestern University Press, 1966.
— *Freud and Philosophy: An Essay on Interpretation*. Trans. by Denis Savage. New Haven and London: Yale University Press, 1790.
— *Le conflit des interprétations: essays d'herméneutique*. Paris: aux Editions du Seuil, 1969.
— *Gabriel Marcel et Karl Jaspers*. Paris: Editions du Temps Présent, 1947.
— *History and Truth*. Translated by Charles A. Kelbley. Evanston: Northwestern University Press, 1965.
— *Husserl: An Analysis of His Phenomenology*. Evanston: Northwestern University Press, 1967.
— *Philosophie de la volonté*. Vol. I: Le Volontaire et l'involontaire. Paris: Aubier, 1950.
— *Philosophie de la volonté*. Vol. II: Finitude et culpabilité: 1. L'homme faillible, 2. La symbolique du mal. Paris: Aubier, 1960.
— *The Symbolism of Evil*. Translated by Emerson Buchanan. New York, Evanston, and London: Harper and Row, 1967.

— "Christianity and the Meaning of History," *Journal of Religion*, Vol. XXXII (1952).
— "Faith and Action," *Criterion*, Vol. II (1963).
— "The Hermeneutics of Symbols and Philosophical Reflection," *International Philosophical Quarterly*, II, No. 2 (1963), 191–218.
— "Herméneutique et réflexion," *Demitizzazone E Immagine*. Padova Cedam-Casa Editrice Dott. Antonio Milani, 1962, 17–41.
— 'Kant and Husserl," *Philosophy Today*, X, Nos. 3–4 (Fall, 1966), 147–68.
— "Le symbole donne à penser," *Esprit*, 1959.
— "New Developments in Phenomenology in France: The Phenomenology of Language," *Social Research*, XXXIV (Spring, 1967), 1–30.
— "Symbolique et temporalité," *Ermeneutica E Tradizione*. Roma: Istituto Di Studi Filosofica, 1963, 5–43.
Ricoeur, Paul, and Dufrenne, Mikel. *Karl Jaspers*. Paris: Editions du Seuil. 1947.

SECONDARY SOURCES

Books

Altizer, Thomas J. *Mircea Eliade and the Dialectic of the Sacred*. Philadelphia: The Westminster Press, 1963.
Bachelard, Gaston. *The Poetics of Space*. New York: The Orion Press, 1964.
Brauer, Jerald C., ed. *The History of Religions*. Chicago and London: The University of Chicago Press, 1967. Vol. I.
Cassirer, Ernst. *Language and Myth*. New York: Dover Publications Inc., 1946.
— *The Philosophy of Symbolic Forms*. Vol. I: Language. New Haven: Yale University Press, 1953.
— *The Philosophy of Symbolic Forms*. Vol. II: Mythical Thought. New Haven: Yale University Press, 1955.
— *The Philosophy of Symbolic Forms*. Vol. III: The Phenomenology of Knowledge. New Haven: Yale University Press, 1957.
Chisholm, Roderick, ed. *Realism and the Background of Phenomenology*. New York: The Free Press, 1960.
Chomsky, Noam. *Aspects of the Theory of Syntax*. Cambridge: Massachusetts Institute of Technology Press, 1965.
Dufrenne, Mikel. *The Notion of the A Priori*. Evanston: Northwestern University Press, 1966.
Edie, James M., ed. *An Invitation to Phenomenology*. Chicago: Quadrangle, 1965.
Eliade, Mircea. *Cosmos and History*. New York: Harper and Row, 1959.
— *Myth and Reality*. New York: Harper and Row, 1963.
— *Patterns in Comparative Religion*. Cleveland: Meridian, 1963.
— *The Sacred and the Profane*. New York: Harcourt, Brace and Co., 1959.
— *Traité d'histoire des religions*. Paris: Payot, 1964.
— *Yoga*. New York: Bollingen Foundation, 1958.
Foucault, Michel. *Les mots et les choses*. Paris: Gallimard, 1966.
Freud, Sigmund. *The Interpretation of Dreams*. New York: Basic Books, Inc., 1959.
Funk, Robert W. *Language, Hermeneutic, and Word of God*. New York: Harper and Row, 1966.
Hamilton, William. *The New Essence of Christianity*. New York: Association Press, 1961.

Harnack, Adolf. *What is Christianity?* New York: Harper and Brothers, 1957.
Harris, Zellig S. *Structural Linguistics.* Chicago: The University of Chicago Press, 1951.
Heidegger, Martin. *Being and Time.* New York: Harper and Row, 1962.
— *Existence and Being.* Chicago: Henry Regnery Co., 1949.
— *An Introduction to Metaphysics.* Garden City: Doubleday and Company Inc., 1959.
Husserl, Edmund. *Cartesian Meditations.* Translated by Dorion Cairns. The Hague: Martinus Nijhoff, 1960.
— *Ideas.* New York: Collier Books, 1962.
— *Phenomenology and the Crisis of Philosophy.* Translated by Quentin Lauer. (Harper Torchbook.) New York, Evanston, and London: Harper and Row, 1965.
— *The Phenomenology of Internal Time-Consciousness.* Bloomington: Indiana University Press, 1964.
Ihde, Donald. *Hermeneutic Phenomenology: The Philosophy of Paul Ricoeur.* Evanston: Northwestern University Press, 1970.
"Paul Ricoeur's Phenomenological Methodology and Philosophical Anthropology." Unpublished Ph.D. dissertation, Boston University Graduate School, 1964. Ann Arbor: University Microfilms, Inc.
Jaspers, Karl. *Truth and Symbol.* New York: Twayne Publishers, 1959.
Jensen, Adolf E. *Myth and Cult Among Primitive Peoples.* Chicago: University of Chicago Press, 1963.
Johnson, F. Ernest. *Religious Symbolism.* New York: The Institute for Religious and Social Studies, 1955.
Kegley, Charles W., ed. *The Theology of Rudolf Bultmann.* New York: Harper and Row Publishers, 1966.
Kierkegaard, Soren. *Concluding Unscientific Postcript.* Princeton: Princeton University Press, 1941.
Lacan, Jaques. *Écrits.* Paris: Aux Éditions du Seuil, 1966.
Langan, Thomas. *Critique of Reason.* New Haven: Yale University Press, 1966.
Langer, Susanne K. *Feeling and Form.* New York: Charles Scribner's Sons, 1953.
— *Philosophy in a New Key.* New York: The New American Library, 1942.
— *Philosophical Sketches.* New York: The New American Library, 1964.
Laszlo, Ervin. *Beyond Scepticism and Realism.* The Hague: Martinus Nijhoff, 1966.
Lauer, Quentin. *Phenomenology: Its Genesis and Prospect.* New York: Harper and Row, 1965.
Lee, Edward N., and Mandelbaum, Maurice, eds. *Phenomenology and Existentialism.* Baltimore: The Johns Hopkins Press, 1967.
Levi-Strauss, Claude. *Structural Anthropology.* New York: Basic Books, 1963.
Levy-Bruhl, Lucien. *Primitive Mentality.* Translated by Lilian A. Clare. Boston: Beacon Press, 1966.
Littleton, C. Scott. *The New Comparative Mythology.* Los Angeles: University of California Press, 1966.
Luckmann, Thomas. *The Invisible Religion.* New York: The Macmillan Co., 1967.
MacQuarrie, John. *An Existentialist Theology.* London: SCM Press Ltd., 1955.
— *The Scope of Demythologizing.* New York: Harper and Brothers, 1960.
Marcel, Gabriel. *Metaphysical Journal.* Chicago: Henry Regnery Co., 1952.
— *The Mystery of Being.* Vol. I: Reflection and Mystery. Chicago: Henry Regnery Co., 1960.
— *The Mystery of Being.* Vol. II: Faith and Reality. Chicago: Henry Regnery Co., 1960.

Ogden, Schubert M. *Christ without Myth*. New York: Harper and Brothers, 1961.
Owen, H. P. *Revelation and Existence*. Cardiff: University of Wales Press, 1957.
Otto, Rudolf. *The Idea of the Holy*. New York: Oxford University Press, 1958.
Perrin, Norman. *Rediscovering the Teaching of Jesus*. New York: Harper and Row, 1967.
Romero, Francisco. *Theory of Man*. Los Angeles: University of California Press, 1964.
Sartre, Jean-Paul. *Being and Nothingness*. New York: Washington Square Press, 1966.
de Saussure, Ferdinand. *Course in General Linguistics*. New York: Philosophical Library, 1959.
Schleiermacher, Friedrich. *On Religion: Speeches to its Cultured Despisers*. (Harper Torchbook.) New York: Harper and Row, 1958.
— *The Christian Faith*. Edinburgh: T. and T. Clark, 1928.
Sebeok, Thomas A. *Myth: A Symposium*. Bloomington: Indiana University Press, 1955.
Spiegelberg, Herbert. *The Phenomenological Movement*. 2 vols. 2d ed. The Hague: Martinus Nijhoff, 1965.
Thévenaz, Pierre. *What is Phenomenology?* Edited by James M. Edie. Chicago: Quadrangle Books Inc., 1962.
Van Buren, Paul M. *The Secular Meaning of the Gospel*. New York: The Macmillan Co., 1963.
van der Leeuw, G. *Religion in Essence and Manifestation*. Vols. I and II. New York: Harper and Row, 1963.
Versenyi, Laszlo. *Heidegger, Being, and Truth*. New Haven: Yale University Press, 1965.
Wittgenstein. Ludwig. *Philosophical Investigations*. New York: The Macmillan Co., 1953.
— *Tractatus Logico-Philosophicus*. New York: The Humanities Press, 1961.

Articles

Altizer, Thomas, J. J. "Mircea Eliade and the Recovery of the Sacred," *The Christian Scholar*, XLV, No. 4 (Winter, 1962), 267–89.
Dardel, Eric. "The Mythic," *Diogenes*, No. 7 (Summer, 1954), 33–51.
Eliade, Mircea. "Crisis and Renewal in History of Religions," *History of Religions*, V, No. 1 (Summer, 1965), 1–17.
— "Cultural Fashions and History of Religions, *"Monday Evening Papers* (Center for Advanced Studies – Wesleyan University), No. 8 (May, 1966).
— "History of Religions and a New Humanism," *History of Religions*, I, No. 1 (Summer, 1961), 1–8.
— "The History of Religions in Retrospect: 1912–1962," *The Journal of Bible and Religion*, XXXI, No. 2 (April, 1963), 98–109.
— "Paradis et Utopie: Géographie mythique et Eschatologie," Extrait De *Eranos-Jahrbuch*, XXXII, (1963), 211–34.
— "The Quest for the 'Origins' of Religion," *History of Religions*, IV, No. 1 (Summer, 1964), 154–69.
Ihde, Donald. "From Phenomenology to Hermeneutic," *The Journal of Existentialism*. Vol. VIII, No. 30, Winter 1967–68, 111–132.
— "Rationality and Myth," *The Journal of Thought*. Vol. 2, No. 1, January 1967, 10–18.

— "Some Parallels Between Analysis and Phenomenology," *Philosophy and Phenomenological Research*, Vol. XXVII, No. 4, June 1967, pp. 577–586.

Perrin, Norman. "The Challenge of New Testament Theology Today," *Criterion*, Vol. IV, No. 2 (Spring, 1965).

Progoff, Ira. "Culture and Being: Mircea Eliade's Studies in Religion," *International Journal of Parapsychology*, III (1961), 47–60.

Rasmussen, David. "Mircea Eliade: Structural Hermeneutics and Philosophy," *Philosophy Today*, Vol. 12, No. 214, Summer 1967.

— "Myth, Structure and Interpretation," *The Origin of Cosmos and Man*, Rome: Studia Missionalia, Vol. xviii, 1969, ed. M. Dhvamony.

— "Ricoeur: The Anthropological Necessity of a Special Language," *Continuum*, Vol. 7, No. 1 Winter-Spring, 1969.

Welbon, G. Richard. "Some Remarks on the work of Mircea Eliade," *Acta Philosophica et Theologica*, Roma, 1964. II, 465–92.

INDEX